DECLASSIFIED

Report of Proceedings

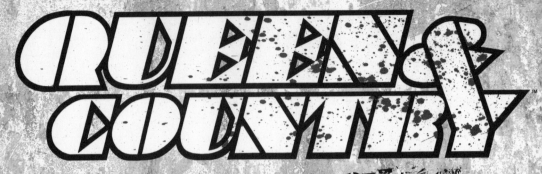

QUEEN & COUNTRY

DECLASSIFIED

Report of Proceedings

compiled by **GREG RUCKA**

illustrated by **BRIAN HURTT**

covers and chapter breaks by
SCOTT MORSE

lettering by
JOHN DRANSKI

introduction by
MICAH IAN WRIGHT

book design by
KEITH WOOD

collection edited by
JAMES LUCAS JONES

original series edited by
**JAMIE S. RICH &
JAMES LUCAS JONES**

Published by Oni Press, Inc.
JOE NOZEMACK, publisher
JAMIE S. RICH, editor in chief
JAMES LUCAS JONES, associate editor
IAN SHAUGHNESSY, editorial intern

Original Queen & Country logo designed by
STEVEN BIRCH @ Servo

This collects issues 1-3 of the Oni Press comics series *Queen & Country™:Declassified*.

ONI PRESS, INC.
6336 SE Milwaukie Avenue, PMB30
Portland, OR 97202
USA

www.onipress.com

First edition: July 2003
ISBN 1-929998-58-9

1 3 5 7 9 10 8 6 4 2

PRINTED IN CANADA

INTRODUCTION
by MICAH WRIGHT

You hold in your hands the fourth volume of *Queen & Country*. This collects the *Declassified* storyline, a side-step out of the chronological order of the rest of the series. This story takes the reader back to 1986 when our heroine Tara Chace was probably listening to Adam and the Ants and hating her parents. It tells a story of Tara's boss, Paul Crocker, in his mid-20's running around East Berlin and Prague in 1986, getting shot at and shooting back. In this story, we are treated to the sight of Crocker as a young Minder doing what he now sends poor Tara Chace out to do. In a way, it's both a flashback story for Paul and a flash-forward for poor Tara. As a former Minder promoted to Director of Operations, Paul stands out as the only career model that Tara has... and look what a crap job HE has.

I could blather on and on about what a great writer Greg Rucka is, but you know that already, don't you? After all, you either bought this book or you're standing in a store somewhere getting your greasy paw prints all over someone else's book while you skim this intro. What's wrong with you? Just go buy it, already! It's a great book by a freaking genius! The reason I know in my heart of hearts that Greg Rucka is a freaking genius is because I lived this book. Not as exciting, with no gunplay, and certainly with a happier ending, but close enough to realize that Greg has totally captured the tone and feeling of 1986 Berlin and Prague down to those cities' most excruciating details.

I've been to Berlin three times in my life. The most recent time was in 1994 on business. The two remerged East and West Berlin were well into the process of cleaning up the mess that the Communists had made of the place. New buildings were springing up and The Wall had been almost completely removed except for museum pieces left behind to remind people of the stupidity of their fellow man. All in all, it was an interesting visit, and I look forward to returning someday and seeing the complete reunification and beautification of the city.

My middle trip to Berlin was two months after the Berlin Wall came down in January 1990. Myself and some former Army buddies decided to meet up in Berlin and go across to the East to celebrate living through Operation Just (be)Cause to see the New Year. What better way to celebrate our victory over the Godless Communists, we thought, than to go get drunk in their town. Once we crossed over into the former East Berlin, we met some Russian Spetznaz soldiers whose first Godless Communist question to us was "Hey, American GI! Could you sell us some good boots?" The Russians told us how their unit was so ill-funded and poorly supplied that they were only issued one-shape-fits-all boots... you would soak your new boots in a bubbling cauldron for five hours, then strap these boiling-hot leathery things to your feet and walk around for eight hours, hoping that these "boots" would mold to fit your feet. Can you imagine? No left boot, no right boot... no size 10, 11, 12, etc. -- just one weird amorphous blob-shaped hobnailed boot which was expected to sorta shrink to fit your foot. This was definitely not Niketown. We got completely rip-roaring drunk with those Spetznaz and three days later, we had some 60 pairs of good, steel shanked and toed jump boots to barter with them for any piece of Russian military gear with a Big Red Star on it. While doing the deal at their barracks, they asked if we minded holding off on the trading until after they'd pulled their potatoes. They then went out into a rock-filled field and began to dig potatoes for their dinner.

Now, let me clarify something: the Soviet Spetznaz were the equivalent of our Delta Force, the toughest trained special forces of the former Soviet Union. These men were hardened killers, veterans of the War in Afghanistan, combat-hardened shock troops the type that we'd been trained to expect to come pouring over the Berlin Wall any day, raping and killing, their eyes filled with a hatred of all that is Good. These were the kind of men we'd trained for years to kill... and here were our vicious Godless Communist enemies out in a half-frozen field digging up their dinner. Over the next week, I saw tanks with no treads, jeeps with no tires, jets with no gas, rifles with no bullets and much, much more. I saw enough to quickly realize that the entire "Red Scare," had been just that... a stupid scare designed to provoke fear in the American Public. A fear which would allow the Military Industrial Complex to crank out more and more weaponry on the taxpayer dime, rather than putting our money towards education, health care, or drug treatment. More M1 Abrahams tanks to outfight those treadless Russian T-72's, more B2 bombers to bomb our potato-digging comrades to pieces, more x-ray lasers and kinetic energy "Star Wars" research to keep our skies free of the evil, Godless Commie bombs.

Ever feel that you've been cheated?

My first time in Berlin (and Prague), however, was in 1986 as an enterprising youth of 16. I was a foreign exchange student to Finland at the time. It was winter in Finland, which is the worst time and place to ever find oneself. Finland has 22 hours of darkness per day in the Winter. The sun peeks up over the horizon at 11am, glides straight across the treetops and dips back down behind the horizon again at 1pm. The light hovers around a dim gloomy dusk for a few hours on either side of those magical "sunny" hours, and after a few months, it's just about enough to make you shoot yourself in the face with a speargun. Many Finns do. Well, maybe not with spearguns, but Finland has abnormally high alcoholism and suicide rates, nonetheless. It also has a huge number of people who just say "forget this, let's go winter in the South."

Which is how I ended up in Berlin and Prague in 1986. And which is how I know Greg Rucka is a genius (hah, you never thought I could get back to that, did you?). When my host family announced we were going for holiday in East Germany and Prague, my heart skipped a few beats: "that's Commieland," thought my Reagan-Era programmed teenaged mind, "We're going on a visit to HELL!" Sure enough, it turned out that East Germany pretty much WAS Hell, or as close to it as Western Europe could possibly get in peacetime.

First off, it was dead ugly. During World War Two, the Russians, Americans and British had all taken turns bombing the holy living snot out of Berlin. Then the city was divided into four zones (France got to run the fourth zone, even though they'd never bombed the place--typical), and later, two zones, with the Soviet Union on one side of their wall and the British and French zones being folded into the American zone on the other side of the wall. East and West Berlin. West Berlin built up along the lines of what you'd expect in a Western city with its eyes on the future. East Berlin, however, just took all the rubble of Hitler's Berlin, crushed it into new concrete slabs and vomited forth into the sky huge, ugly, demoralizing tombstones of buildings. Enormous grey things which emphasized the meaninglessness of the individual compared to the awesome power of The State. When I opened the first issue of *Declassified* and got to the 2-page spread of the former no-man's land between East and West Berlin, I was shocked. Brian Hurtt had captured it perfectly. I immediately flashed back to that day when I first laid eyes on "Checkpoint Charlie" and passed through into Commieland with my very own East German Stasi (Secret Police) stalker to follow my host family and I from place to place, visiting distant family and getting a good look at what life under Communism looked like. I don't think I was comfortable for a single second the entire time we were in East Germany. Tellingly, neither was my host family, all of whom had done this trip several times.

Then we hopped into our rented Lada and drove deeper into Commieland... to the dreaded Czechoslovakia. I'm not sure why it was to be dreaded, but somehow, I knew that it was. Again, Brian Hurtt seems to have gotten it perfectly correct... the narrow streets, the twisting alleys, the arched doorways, the ceiling moldings in the rooms, the strange non-Western furniture, the sidewalk cafes. I'll never forget that terrifying trip and the creeping sense of threat that lurked at the edges of my perception. Was that guy looking at us? And what's with that black car that keeps circling the block? And who's this following us on foot into all the stores? Again, in *Declassified*, Greg Rucka does a genius job of setting up the horrible feeling of imposing menace that came with Communism... the idea that at any moment the Secret Police might come kick in your door and haul you off to a prison camp in Cuba for saying or thinking the wrong thing about The Monolithic State. You'd almost think Greg was living in that kind of place now, his depiction of it in these pages is so real and palpable.

Incidentally, I say that as a joke, but I'd like to point out something: when the Berlin Wall fell and the East German Stasi were disbanded, a search of their files turned up some interesting statistics: the Stasi had kept a file on one out of every three citizens of East Germany. One out of every five phones in the country had been tapped. Even more chilling, the Stasi had a network of informers and neighborhood spies more than 300,000 strong -- one in every 56 people was a snitch for the Secret Police. Children were encouraged to snitch out their parents, parents encouraged to spy on their coworkers, coworkers to inform on their spouses, spouses to report anti-communist children, a vicious circle of claim, counterclaim and double-blame. Here in the United States, we have our own Stasi being built... laws like the Patriot Act and the Domestic Security Enhancement Act give the government and their secretive Department of Homeland Security the power to invade our lives, spy on the books we read, tap the calls we make, to search our homes without a warrant while we're not home, to strip us of our citizenship and to deport us to prison camps in Cuba without recourse of a trial or a lawyer. Attorney General John Ashcroft even tried to greenlight a program called "Project TIPS" whereupon all cable TV installers, gas meter readers and bottled water delivery men would be deputized to sneak around your home and to fill out reports on your day to day life.

We stand at the precipice of a fateful decision: to go down the path of East Germany, every citizen a suspect, cameras in every home and on every street corner, or to make a stand against the creeping fascism which threatens to take hold in this country. Let's learn something from the people that Greg is writing about in this book. It was NOT the Paul Crockers of the world who freed the East Germans of the bonds of their tyranny... it was the people themselves. Throughout the summer of 1989, the Communist regime found itself under enormous pressure because huge numbers of East Germans were crossing the border into Hungary, where the regime had torn gaping holes in the Iron Curtain that separated East from West, and then crossing into West Germany. Meanwhile at home in East Germany, many protesters were determined to remain and to fight for the future of their country. "Wir bleiben hier!", "We are staying here!" was a popular chant. It caused even more problems for the authorities. Peaceful demonstrations against the East German regime took place in the months leading up to the fall of the Berlin Wall in 1989. People filled the St. Nicholas church in Leipzig, while tens of thousands gathered outside. The protesters were acting in defiance of State orders not to demonstrate, and even ignored the armed militias standing on street corners. They walked through the city's streets holding candles, chanting: "Wir sind das Volk! Keine Gewalt!", "We are one people! No violence!" For the regime, it was the beginning of the end.

In these times of panic, suspicion and terror, we're constantly told that only a strong and secretive State can protect us from the evil terrorists. Even a cursory read of *Queen & Country* reveals that this is quite simply untrue... these are people who have incredibly complex personal and political agendas, into many of which the Welfare of the Public and our Civil Rights never quite enter into the equation. Secrecy Breeds Tyranny and Dissent Protects Democracy. Any other type of thinking leads us down the road to where we find ourselves patrolling barbed-wire borders with dogs and machine guns, shooting old men in the back of the head as people like Paul Crocker try to save us one at a time from our own cowardice.

Micah Wright
June 24, 2003

After spending four years as an Airborne Ranger in the U. S. Army, Micah Wright took the next logical career step: writing children's animation. His writing credits include the Nick Toons Angry Beavers *and* Sponge Bob Square-Pants, *the military/superhero comic* Stormwatch *for DC/Wildstorm, and a new book,* You Back the Attack, We'll Bomb Who We Want *which features World War II propaganda posters re-mixed into bold statements on the current state of government, freedom, and patriotism in America.*

CHAPTER 1

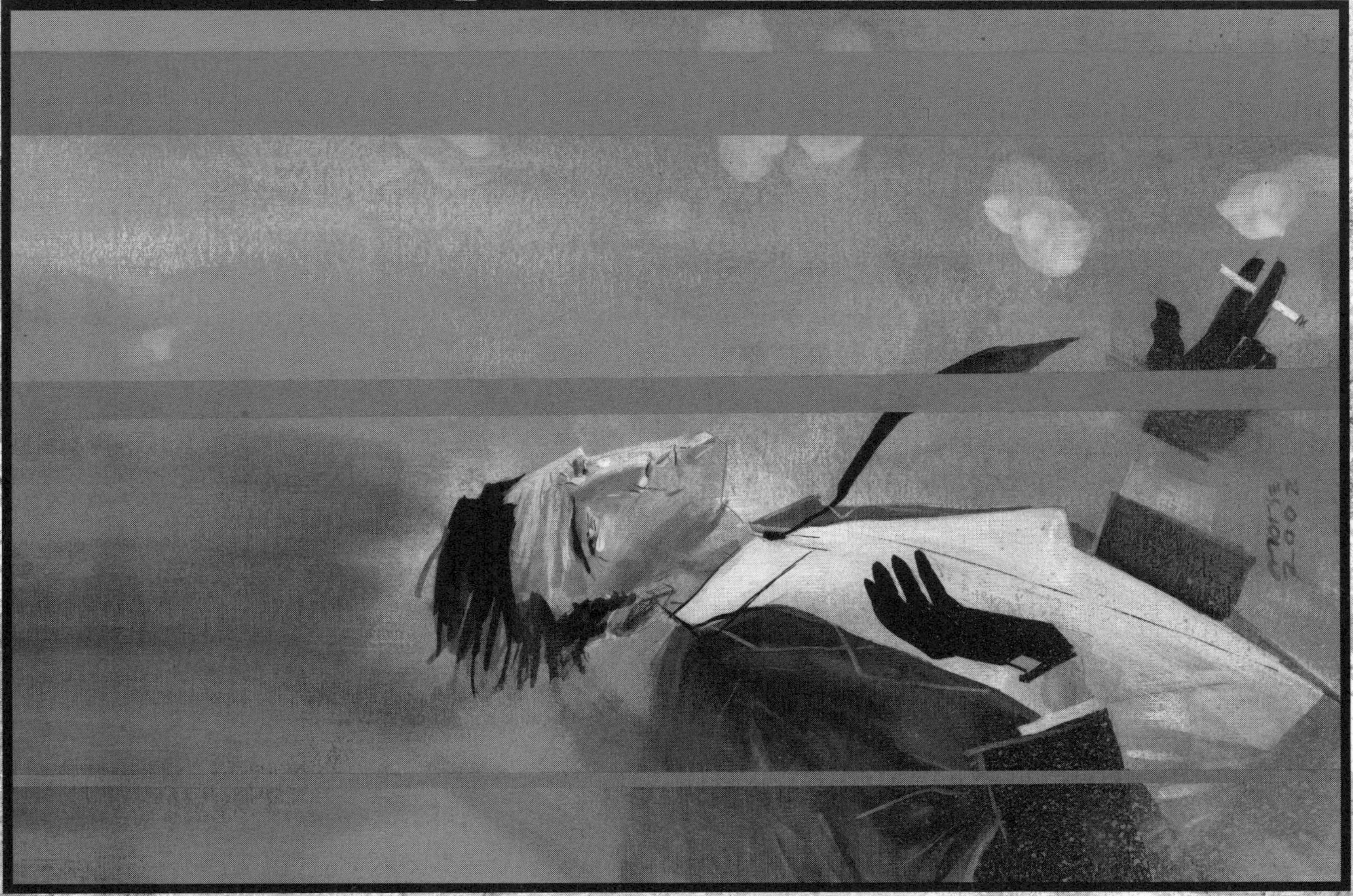

S.I.S.:

JAMES WATSON

Director of Operations for SIS, responsible for all day-to-day operations and intelligence gathering performed by SIS, as well as all "special" operations performed by the Minders.

LINDSAY MILLS

Minder One, eleven year veteran of SIS, head of the Special Operations Division (also known as the Special Section). Considered by many to be one of the best special operations officers working in the world.

WESLEY HARGREAVES

Minder Two, with five years of SIS duty under his belt.

DONALD WELDON

Prague Station Number Two. Acts as gopher and resident legman for the Prague Number One.

PAUL CROCKER

In his mid-twenties, newly married, considered by many at SIS to be a prodigy in the field. The latest addition to the Special Section, with the designation of Minder Three.

JOHN GILCHRIST

Mission Control Officer (also called Main Communications Officer), responsible for maintaining communications between the Operations Room (Ops Room) in London and agents running in the field.

GARY MACHON

Duty Operations Officer, acts as the conduit for all incoming and outgoing information with operational impact. Monitors and evaluates information, as well as implementing the Director of Operations' mission orders.

FRANCES BARCLAY

Frances Barclay, the Prague Station Chief (or Prague Number One). Heads the resident SIS mission in Czechoslovakia.

K.G.B.:

VALERY KARPIN

KGB Resident Officer in Prague, twenty-seven year veteran of the Cold War.

RUSLAN IZMAILOV

KGB Officer, recent addition to the Executive Action division.

OTHERS:

JENNY CROCKER

Jenny Crocker, in her early twenties, wife of Paul. Aware that he works for SIS, but not certain in what capacity. Teaches pre-school.

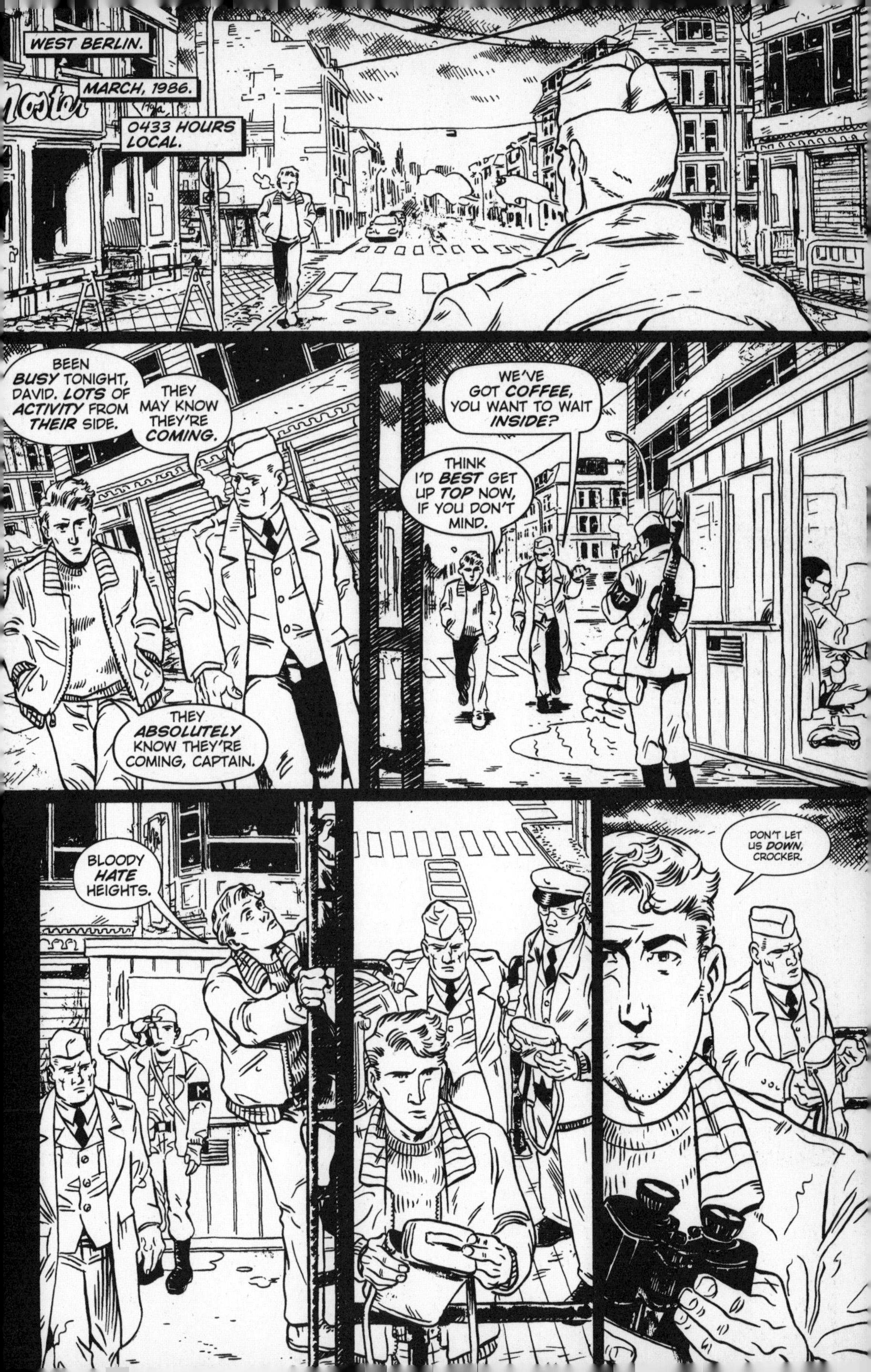
WEST BERLIN.
MARCH, 1986.
0433 HOURS LOCAL.
BEEN BUSY TONIGHT, DAVID. LOTS OF ACTIVITY FROM THEIR SIDE.
THEY MAY KNOW THEY'RE COMING.
THEY ABSOLUTELY KNOW THEY'RE COMING, CAPTAIN.
WE'VE GOT COFFEE, YOU WANT TO WAIT INSIDE?
THINK I'D BEST GET UP TOP NOW, IF YOU DON'T MIND.
BLOODY HATE HEIGHTS.
DON'T LET US DOWN, CROCKER.

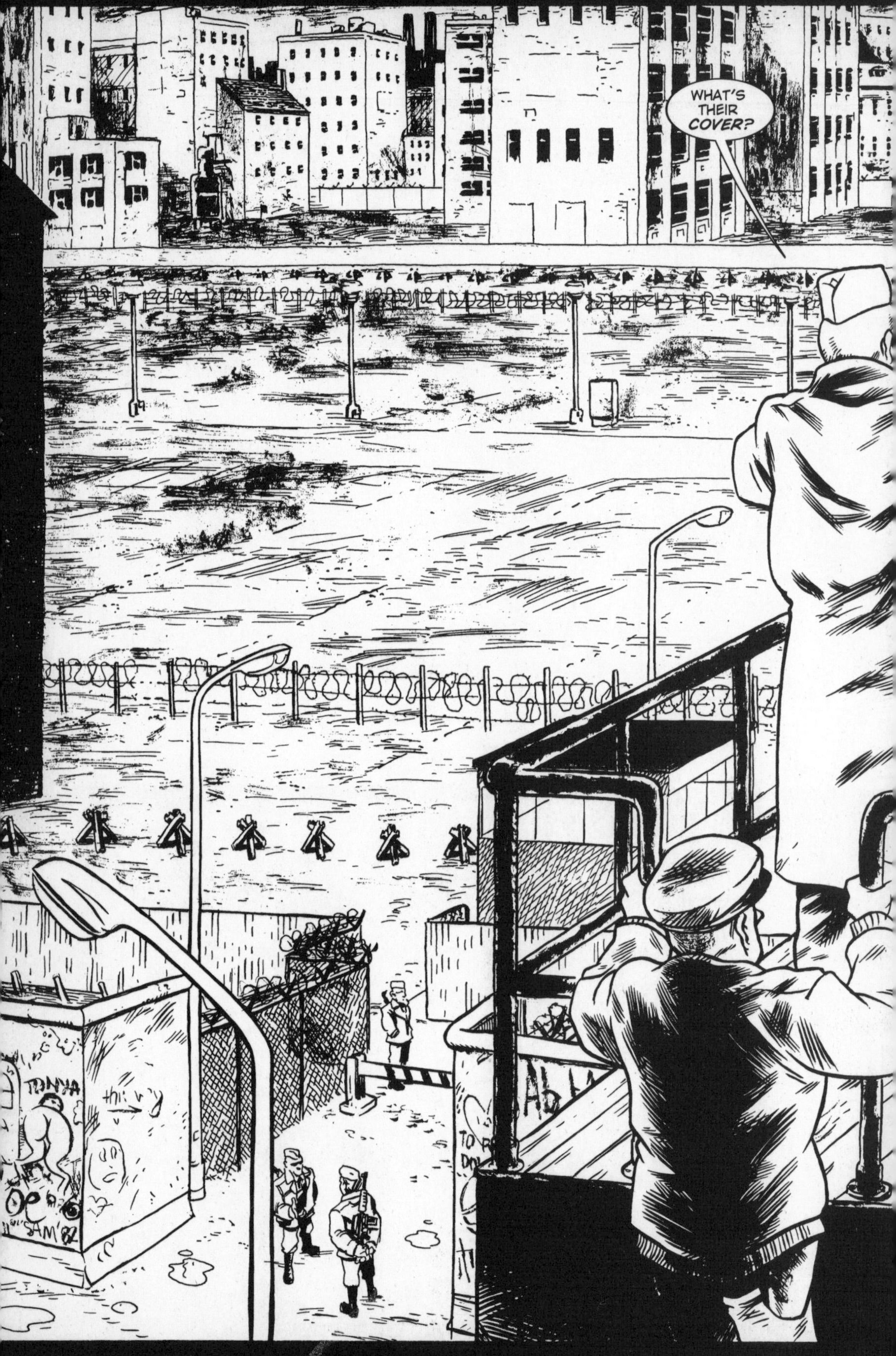
WHAT'S THEIR COVER?

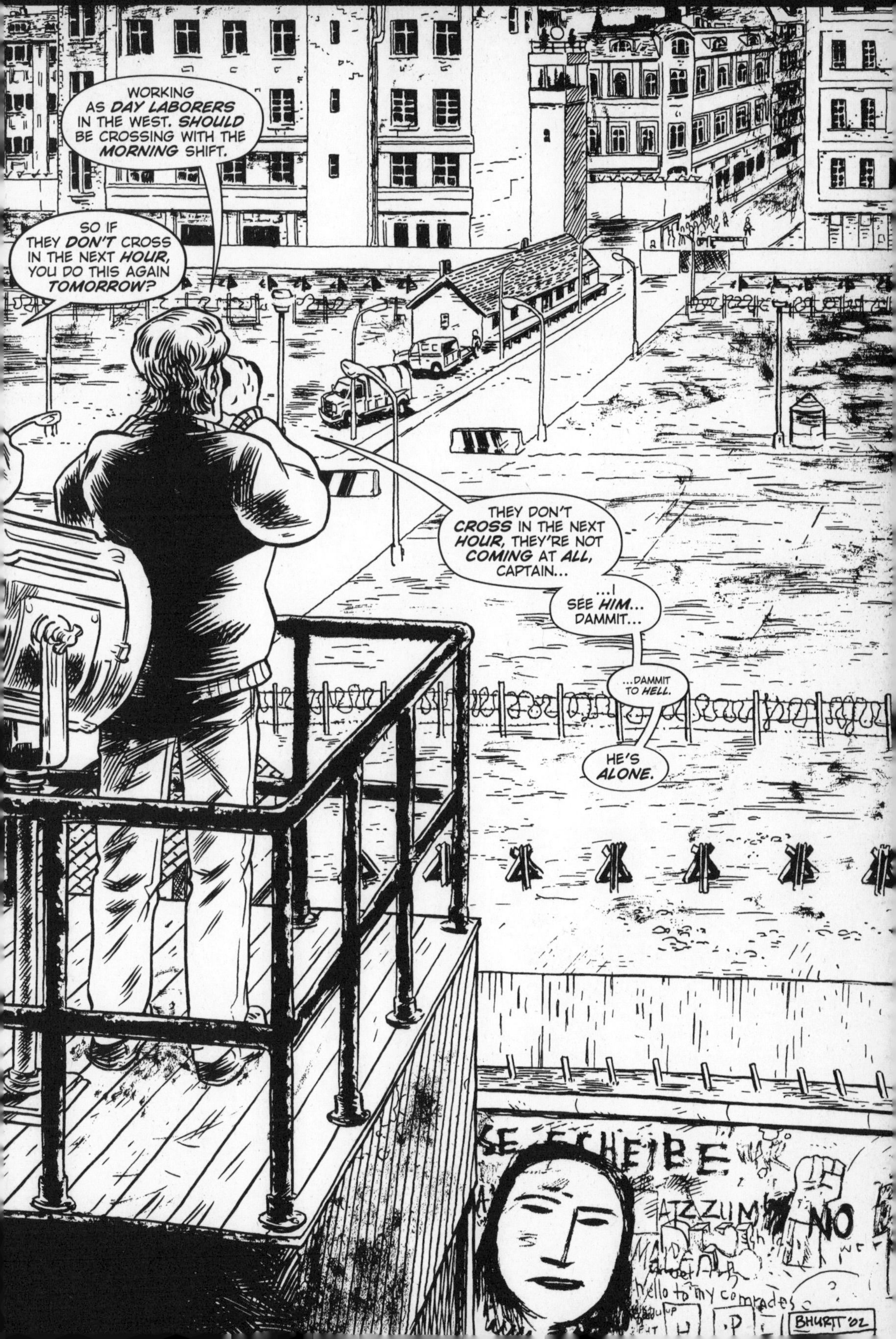

WORKING AS *DAY LABORERS* IN THE WEST. *SHOULD* BE CROSSING WITH THE *MORNING* SHIFT.
SO IF THEY *DON'T* CROSS IN THE NEXT *HOUR,* YOU DO THIS AGAIN *TOMORROW?*
THEY DON'T *CROSS* IN THE NEXT *HOUR,* THEY'RE NOT *COMING* AT *ALL,* CAPTAIN...
...I SEE *HIM*... DAMMIT...
...DAMMIT TO *HELL.*
HE'S *ALONE.*
NO
hello to my comrades
BHURTT '02

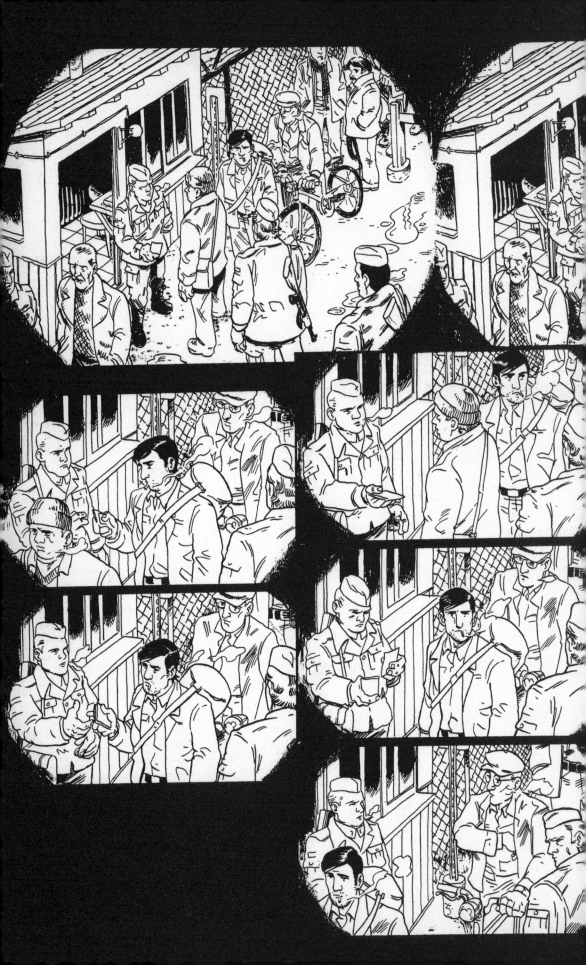

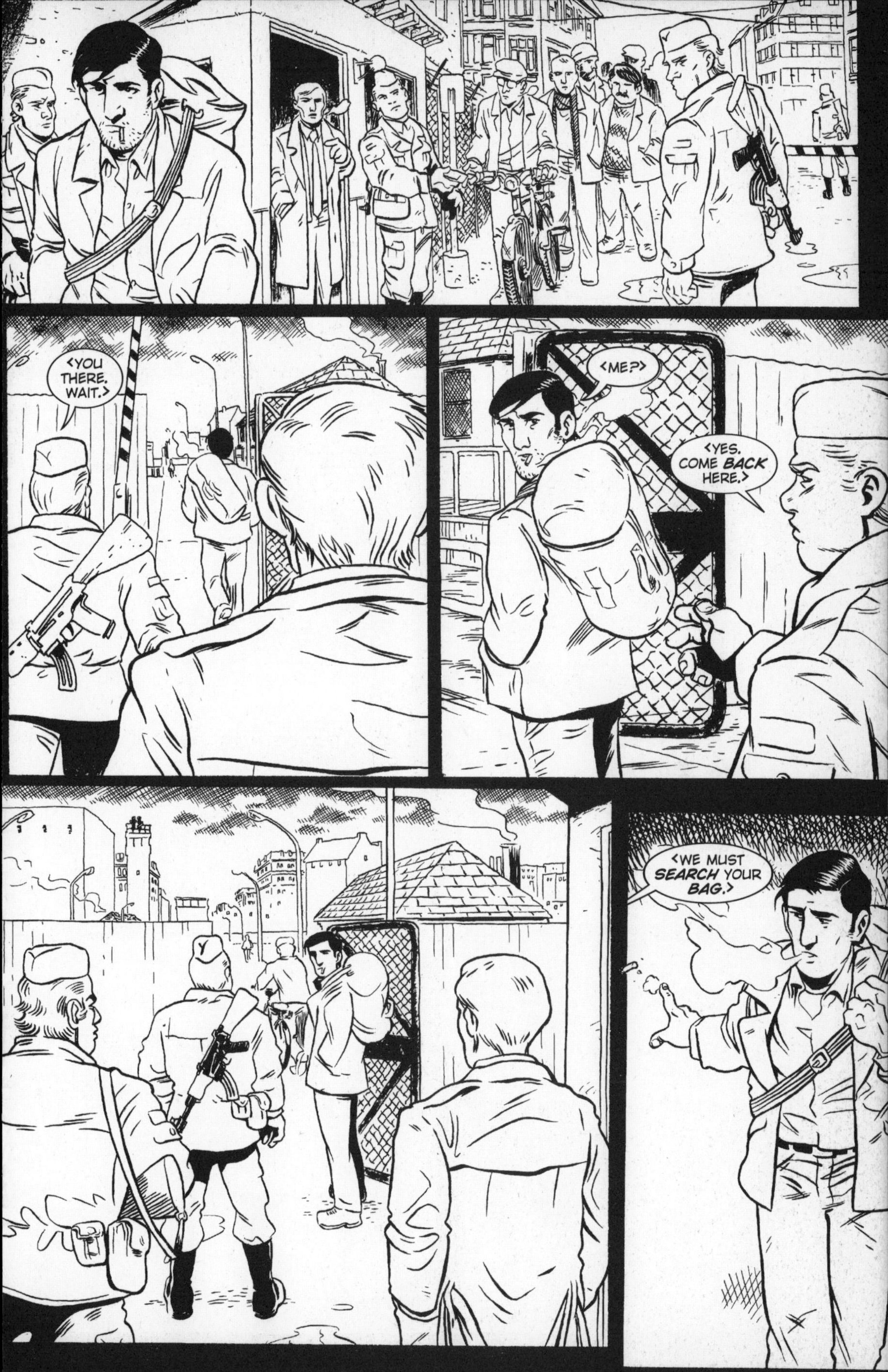

<YOU THERE. WAIT.>
<ME?>
<YES. COME BACK HERE.>
<WE MUST SEARCH YOUR BAG.>

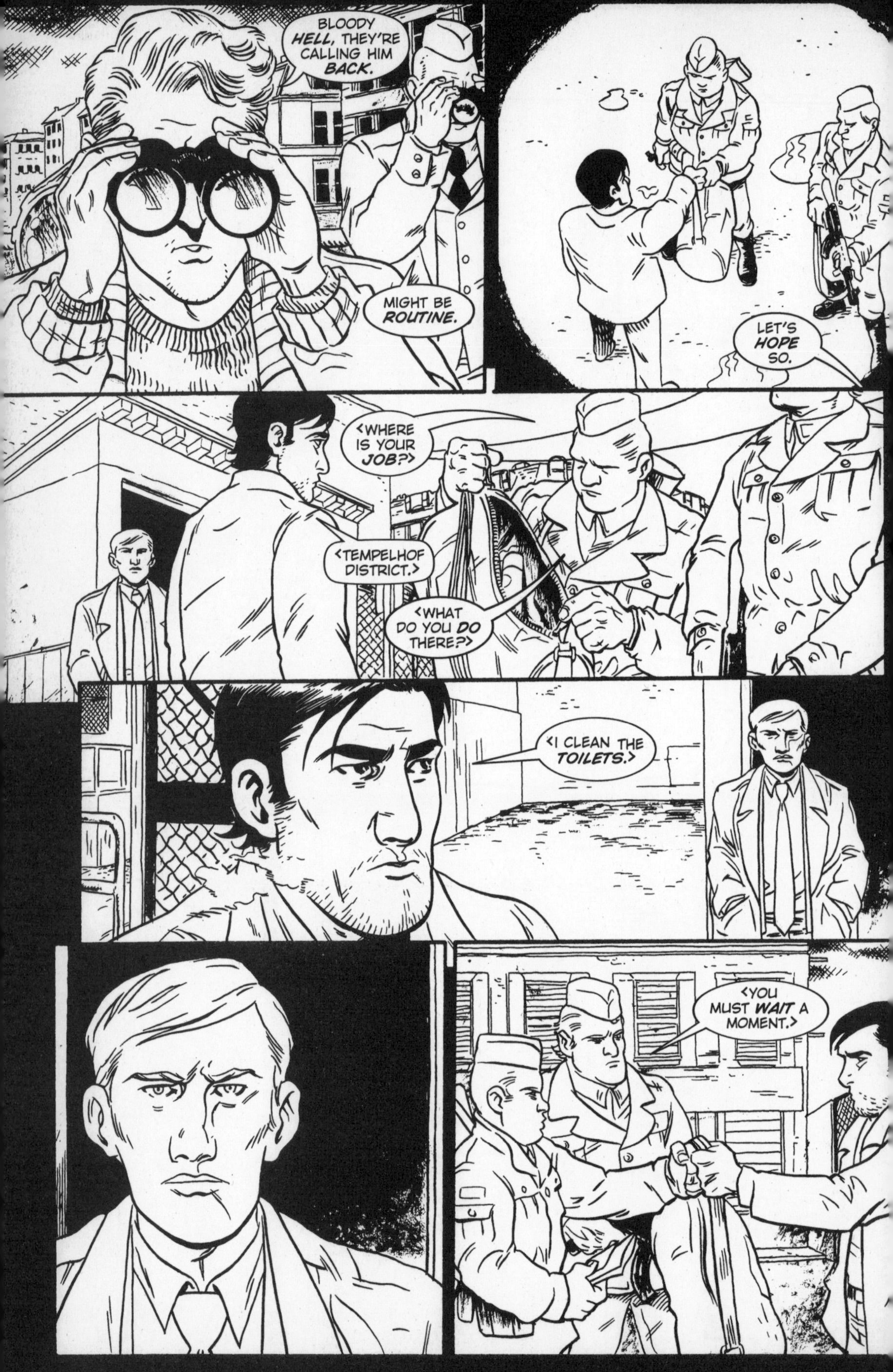
BLOODY HELL, THEY'RE CALLING HIM BACK.
MIGHT BE ROUTINE.
LET'S HOPE SO.
<WHERE IS YOUR JOB?>
<TEMPELHOF DISTRICT.>
<WHAT DO YOU DO THERE?>
<I CLEAN THE TOILETS.>
<YOU MUST WAIT A MOMENT.>

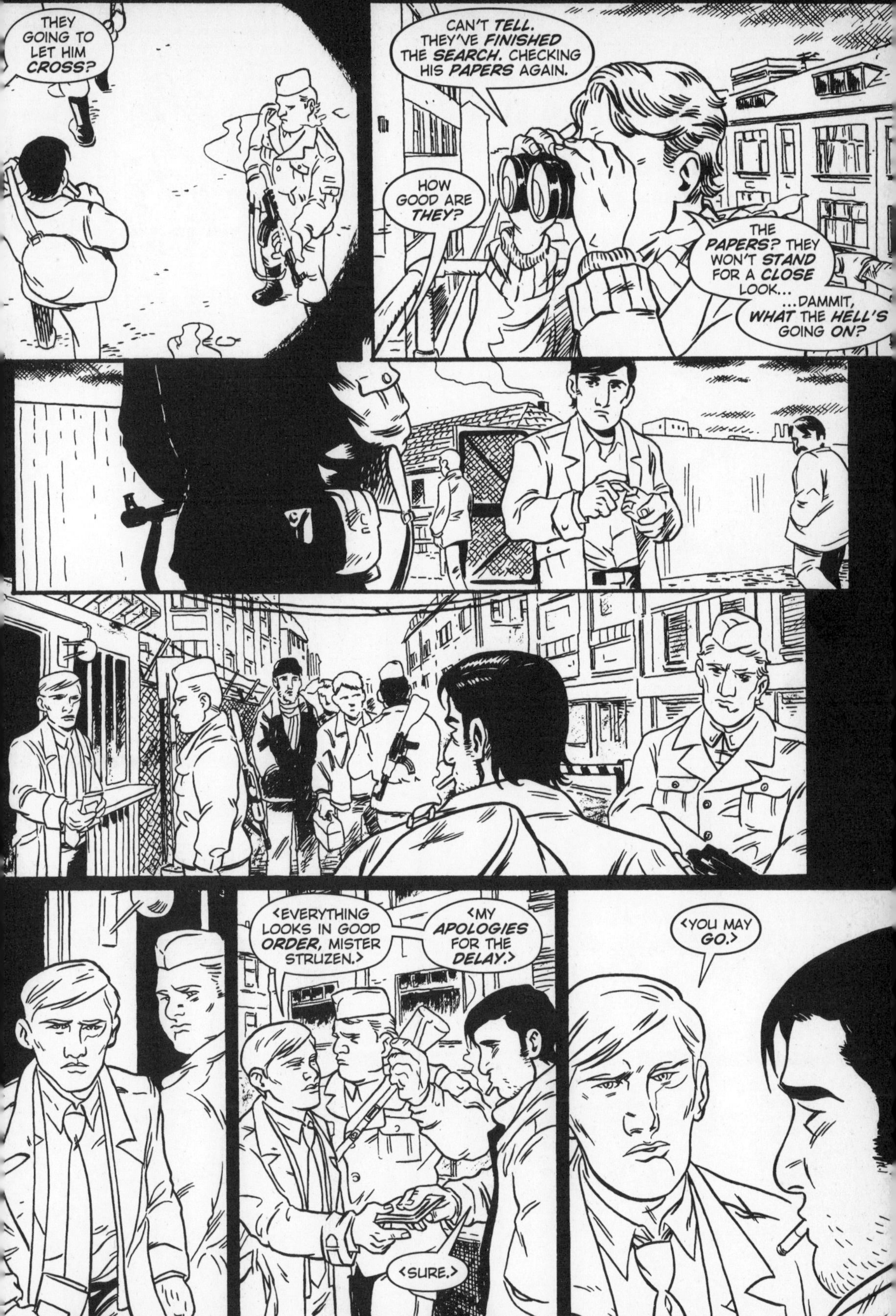
THEY GOING TO LET HIM CROSS?
CAN'T TELL. THEY'VE FINISHED THE SEARCH. CHECKING HIS PAPERS AGAIN.
HOW GOOD ARE THEY?
THE PAPERS? THEY WON'T STAND FOR A CLOSE LOOK...
...DAMMIT, WHAT THE HELL'S GOING ON?
<EVERYTHING LOOKS IN GOOD ORDER, MISTER STRUZEN.>
<MY APOLOGIES FOR THE DELAY.>
<SURE.>
<YOU MAY GO.>

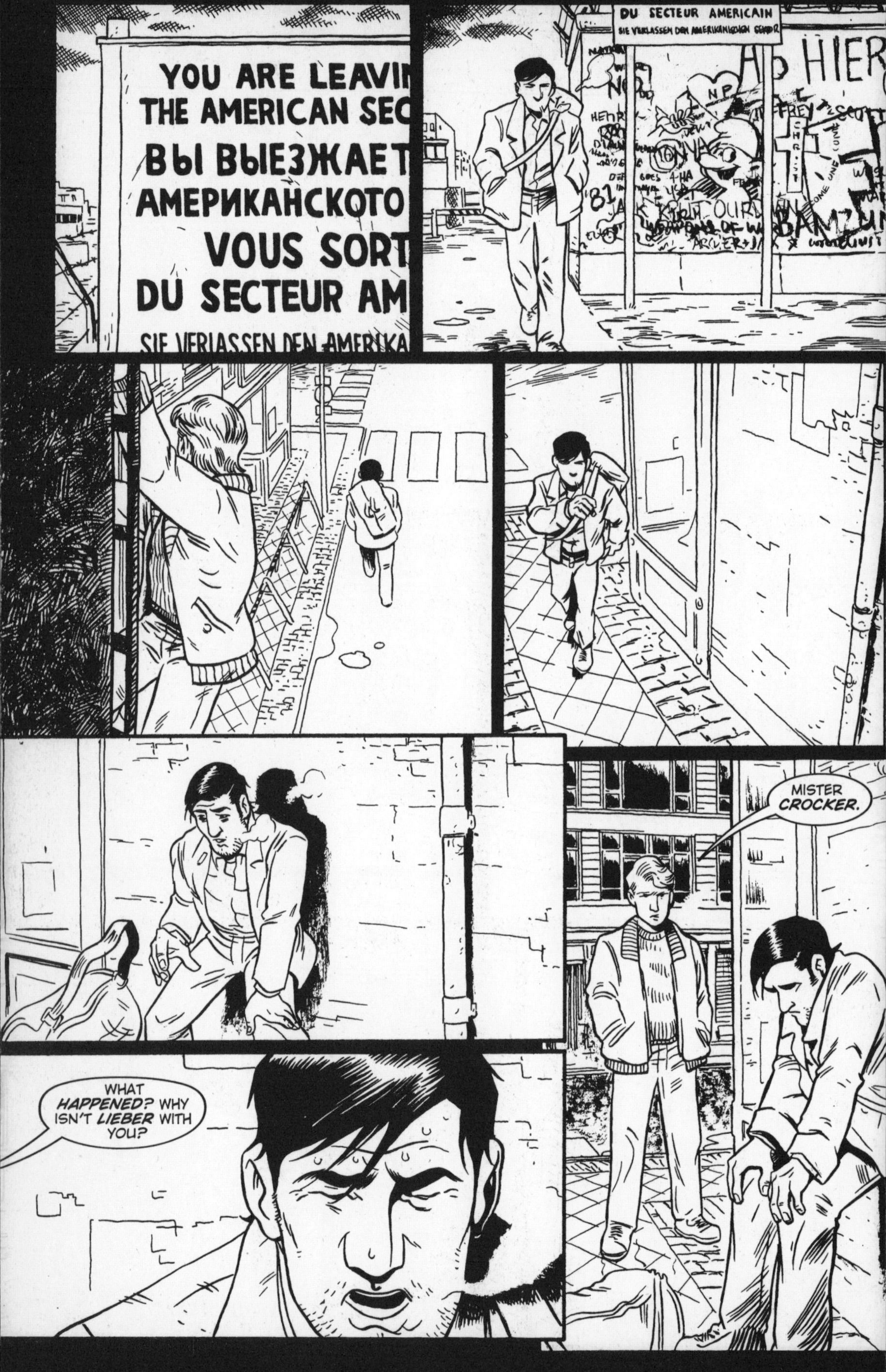
YOU ARE LEAVIN
THE AMERICAN SEC
ВЫ ВЫЕЗЖАЕТ
АМЕРИКАНСКОТО
VOUS SORT
DU SECTEUR AM
SIE VERLASSEN DEN AMERIKA
DU SECTEUR AMERICAIN
MISTER CROCKER.
WHAT HAPPENED? WHY ISN'T LIEBER WITH YOU?

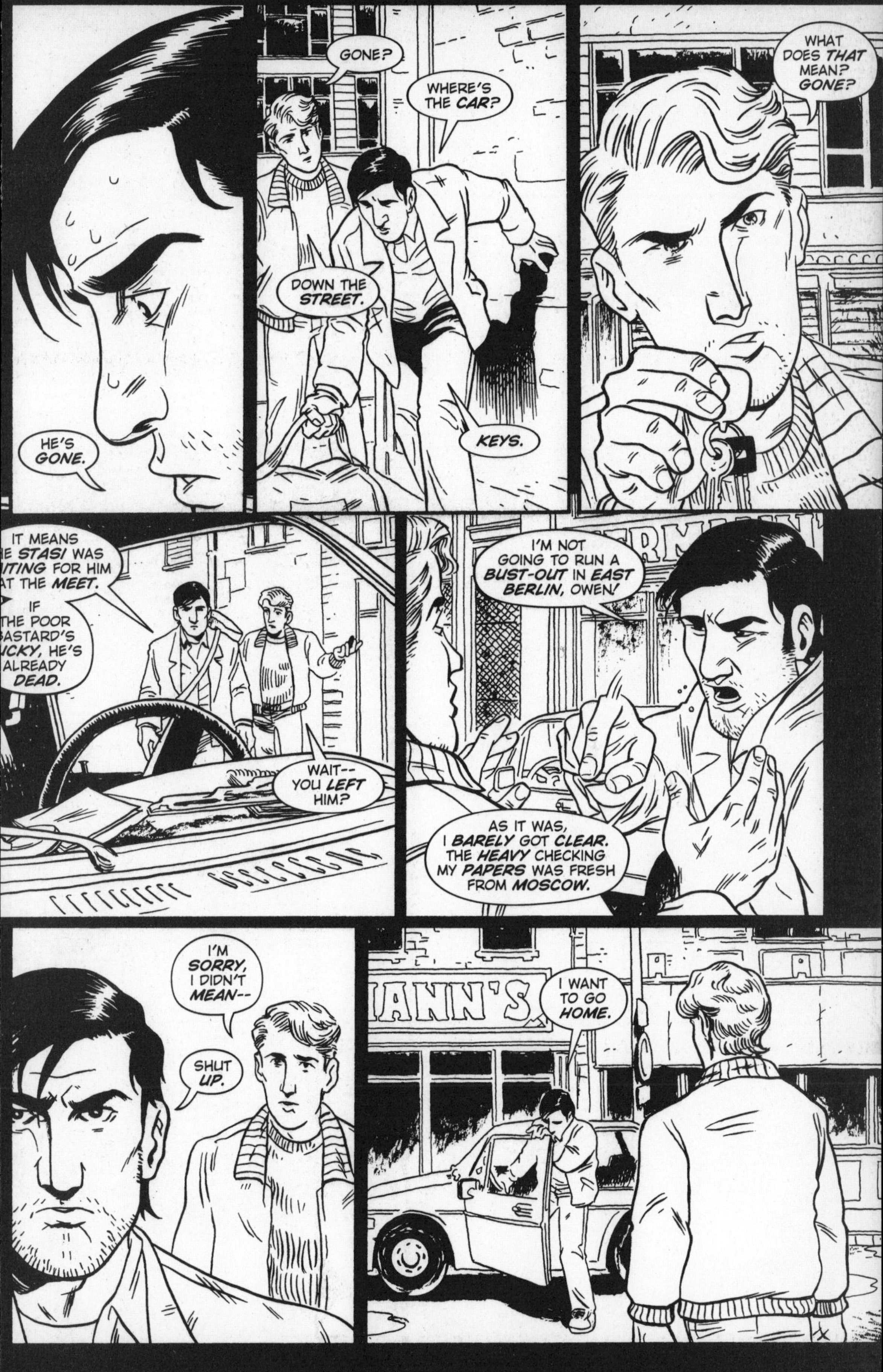
HE'S GONE.
GONE?
WHERE'S THE CAR?
DOWN THE STREET.
KEYS.
WHAT DOES THAT MEAN? GONE?
IT MEANS HE STASI WAS ITING FOR HIM AT THE MEET.
IF THE POOR ASTARD'S UCKY, HE'S ALREADY DEAD.
WAIT-- YOU LEFT HIM?
I'M NOT GOING TO RUN A BUST-OUT IN EAST BERLIN, OWEN!
AS IT WAS, I BARELY GOT CLEAR. THE HEAVY CHECKING MY PAPERS WAS FRESH FROM MOSCOW.
I'M SORRY, I DIDN'T MEAN--
SHUT UP.
I WANT TO GO HOME.

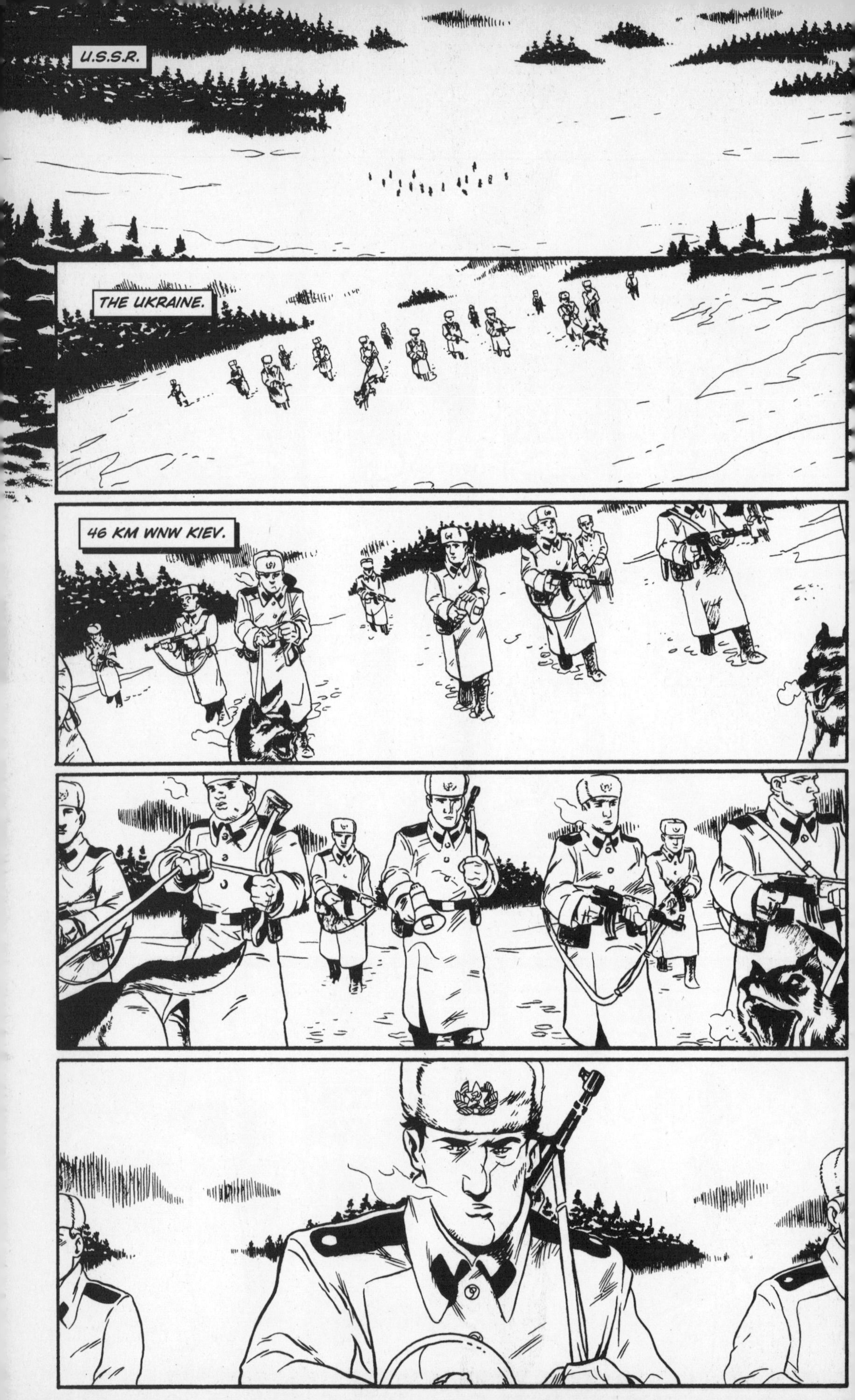
U.S.S.R.
THE UKRAINE.
46 KM WNW KIEV.

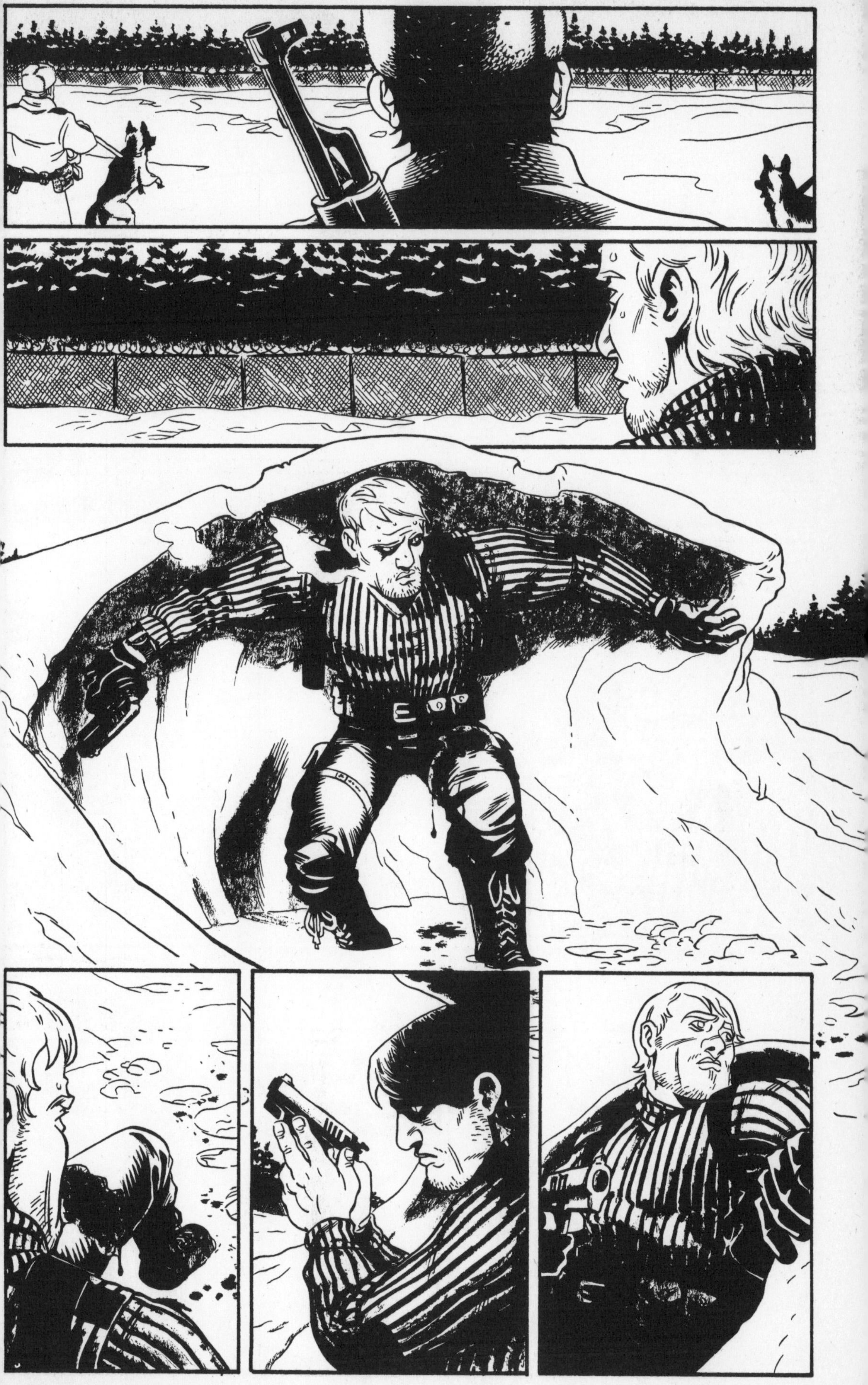

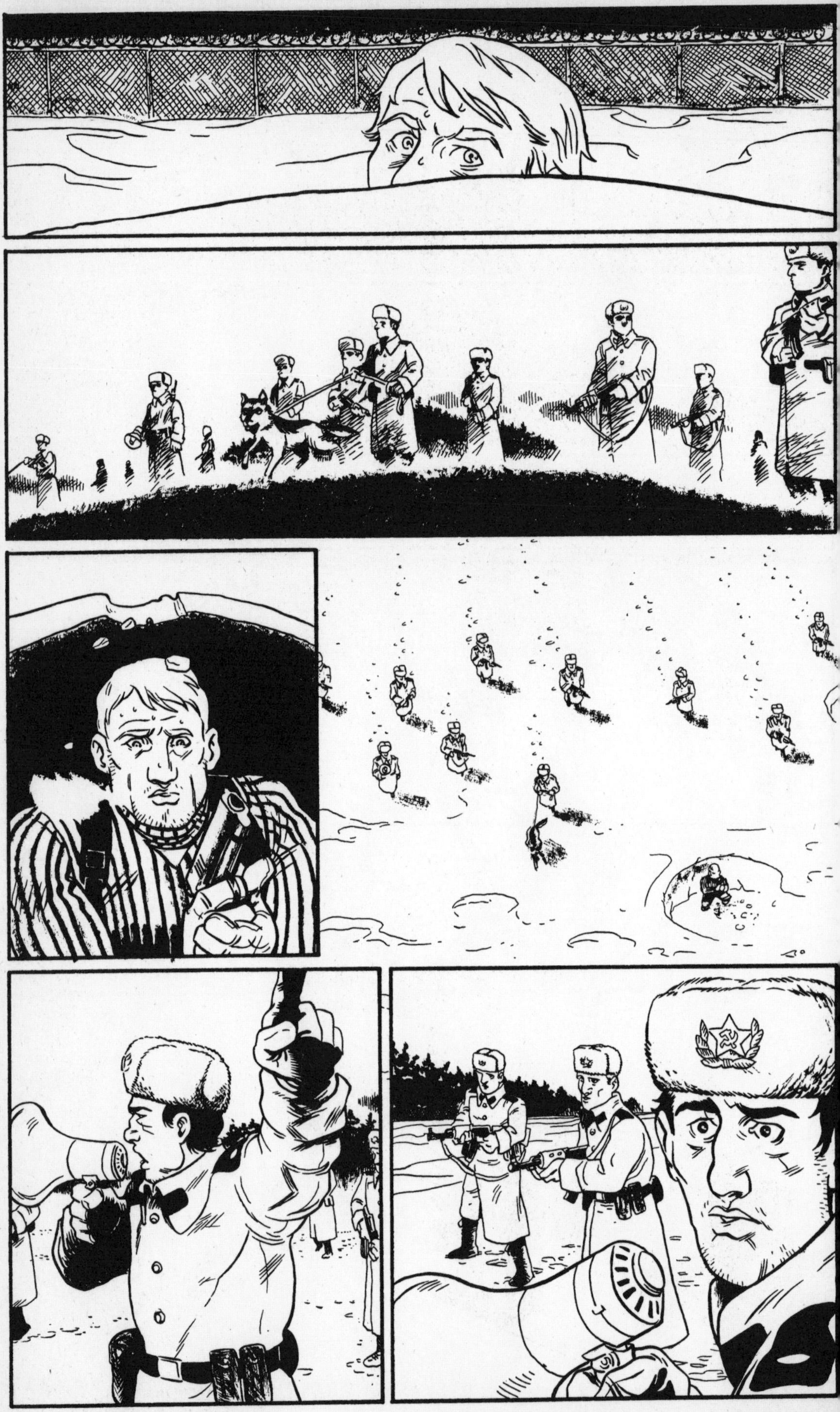

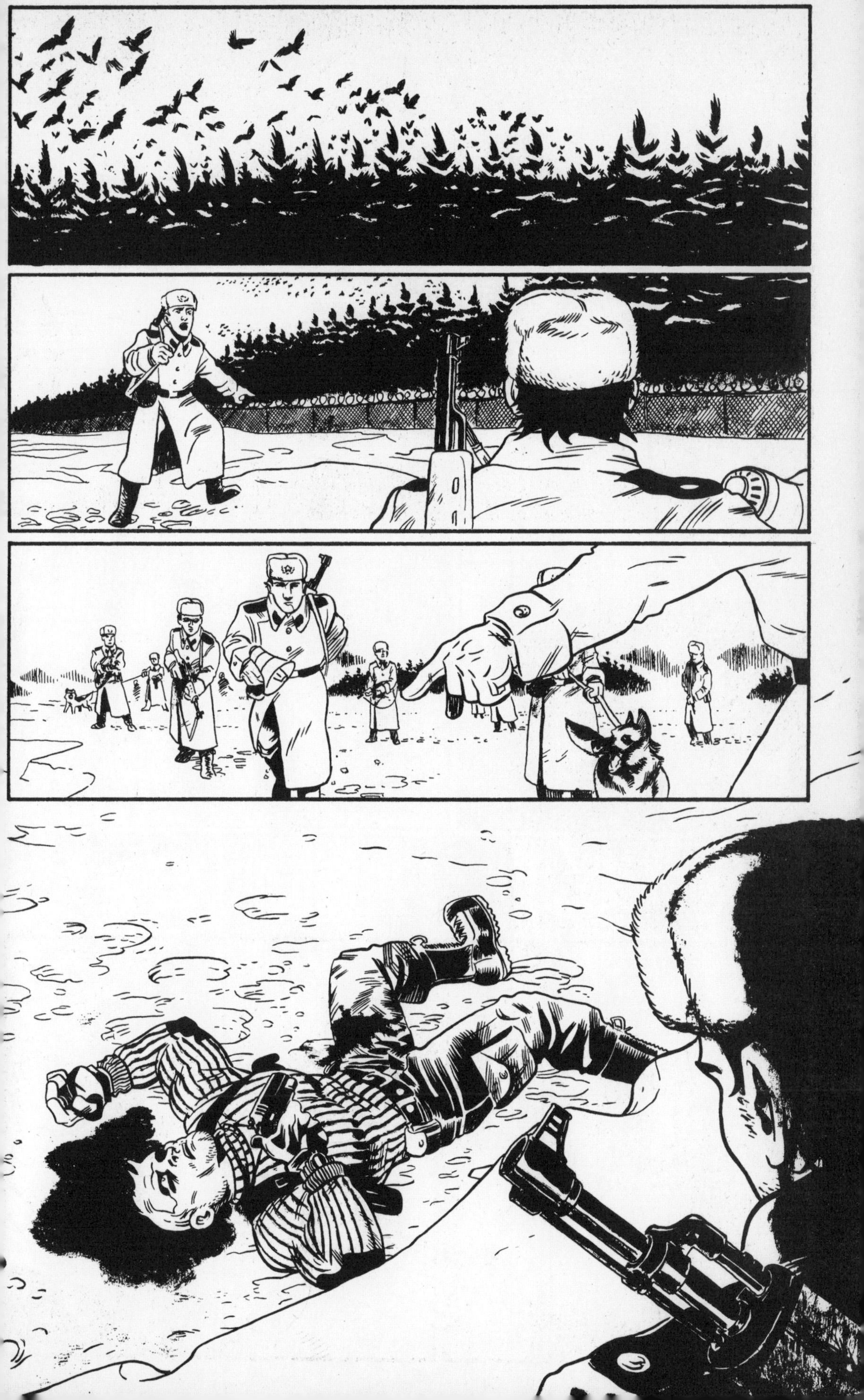

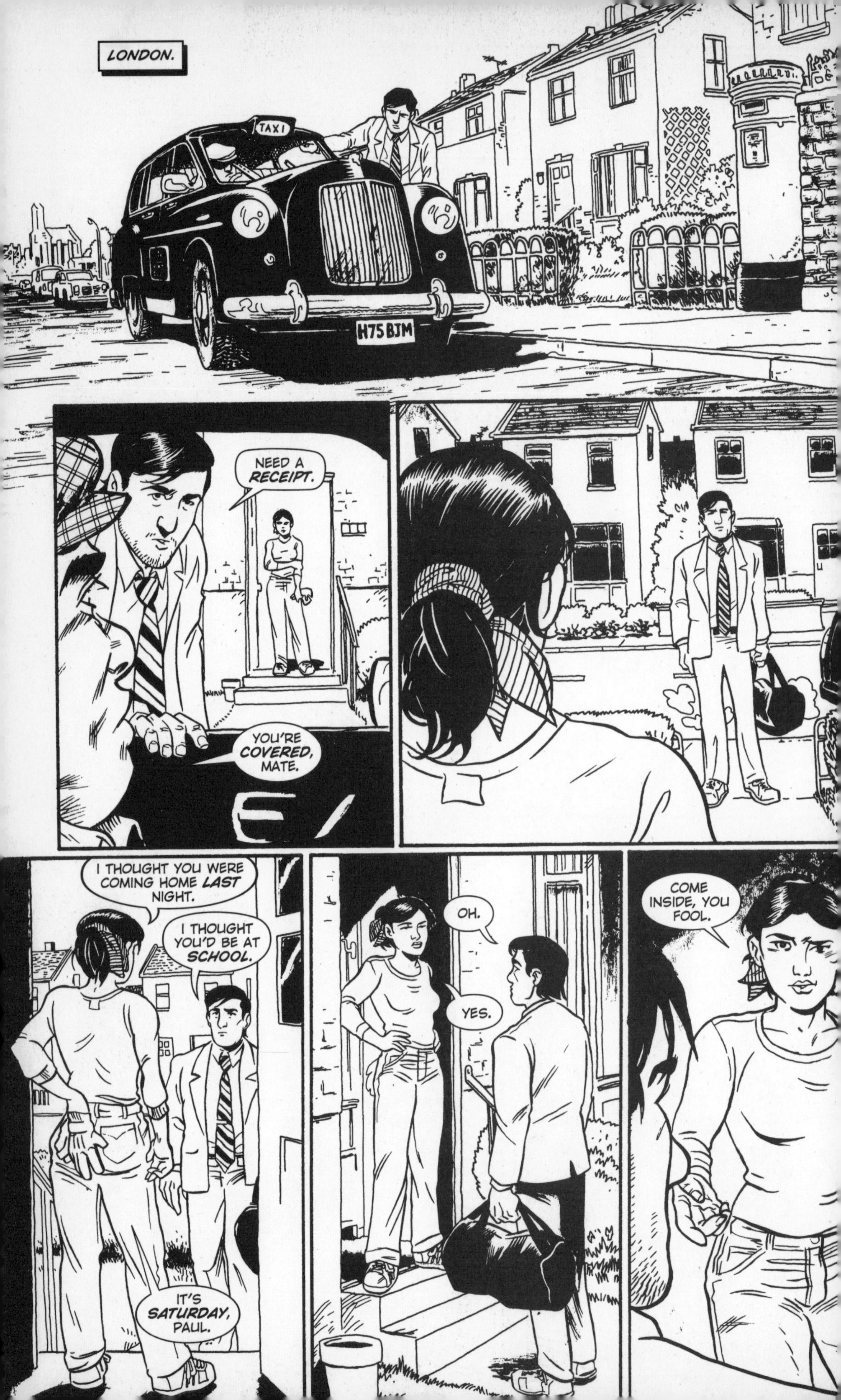
LONDON.
TAXI
H75 BJM
NEED A RECEIPT.
YOU'RE COVERED, MATE.
I THOUGHT YOU WERE COMING HOME LAST NIGHT.
I THOUGHT YOU'D BE AT SCHOOL.
IT'S SATURDAY, PAUL.
OH.
YES.
COME INSIDE, YOU FOOL.

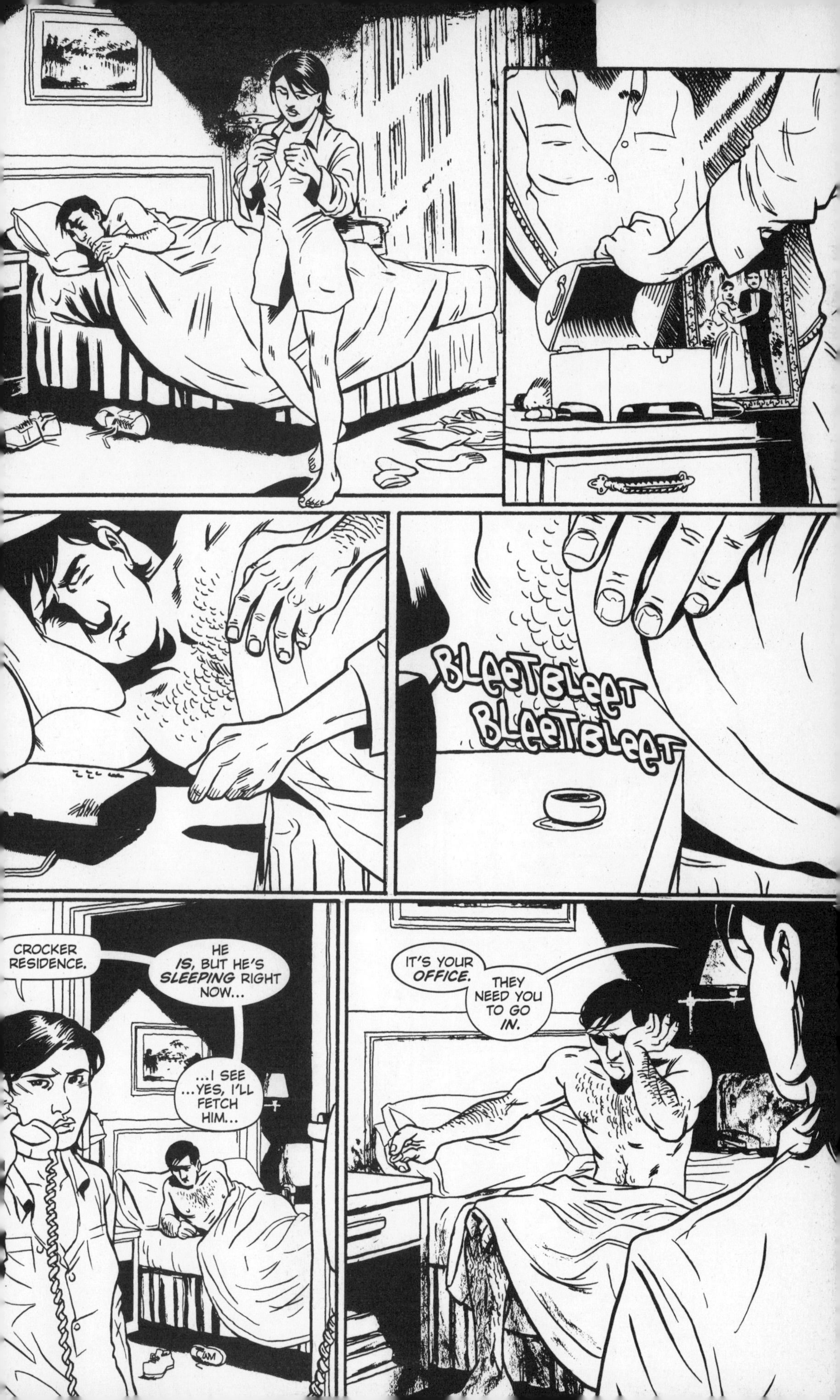
BLEETBLEET
BLEETBLEET
CROCKER RESIDENCE.
HE IS, BUT HE'S SLEEPING RIGHT NOW...
...I SEE ...YES, I'LL FETCH HIM...
IT'S YOUR OFFICE.
THEY NEED YOU TO GO IN.

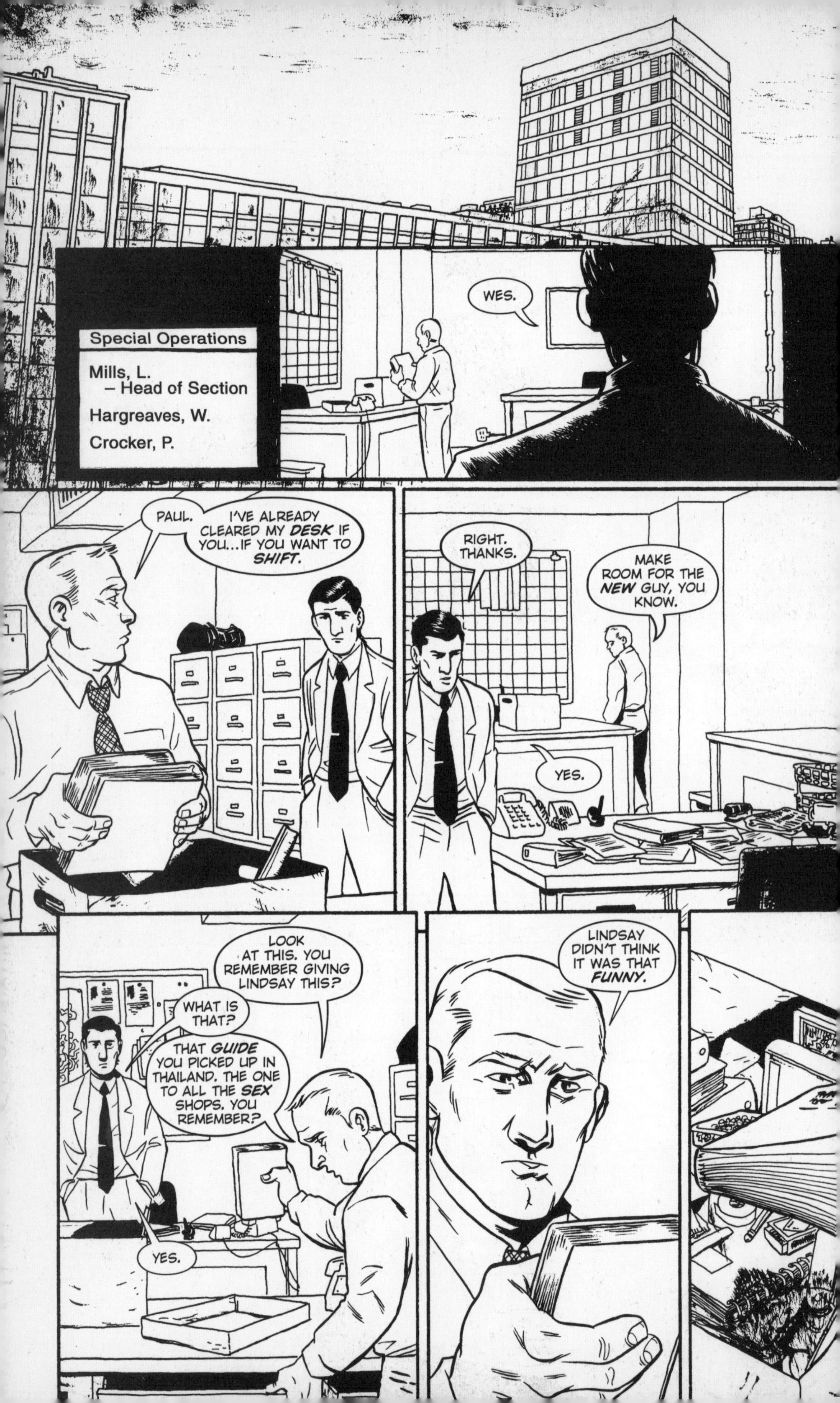
Special Operations
Mills, L. – Head of Section
Hargreaves, W.
Crocker, P.
WES.
PAUL.
I'VE ALREADY CLEARED MY DESK IF YOU...IF YOU WANT TO SHIFT.
RIGHT. THANKS.
MAKE ROOM FOR THE NEW GUY, YOU KNOW.
YES.
LOOK AT THIS. YOU REMEMBER GIVING LINDSAY THIS?
WHAT IS THAT?
THAT GUIDE YOU PICKED UP IN THAILAND. THE ONE TO ALL THE SEX SHOPS. YOU REMEMBER?
YES.
LINDSAY DIDN'T THINK IT WAS THAT FUNNY.

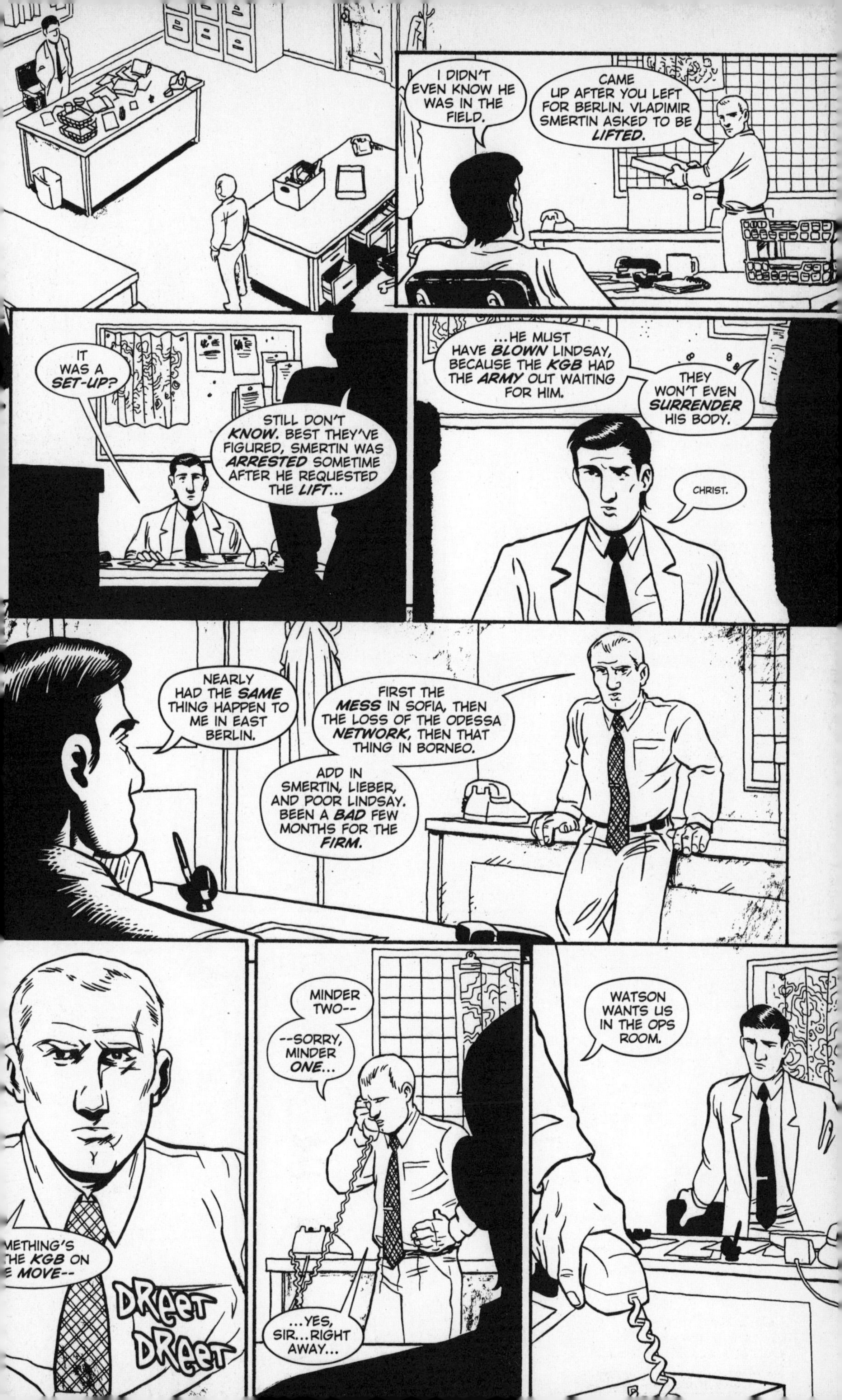
I DIDN'T EVEN KNOW HE WAS IN THE FIELD.
CAME UP AFTER YOU LEFT FOR BERLIN. VLADIMIR SMERTIN ASKED TO BE LIFTED.
IT WAS A SET-UP?
STILL DON'T KNOW. BEST THEY'VE FIGURED, SMERTIN WAS ARRESTED SOMETIME AFTER HE REQUESTED THE LIFT...
...HE MUST HAVE BLOWN LINDSAY, BECAUSE THE KGB HAD THE ARMY OUT WAITING FOR HIM.
THEY WON'T EVEN SURRENDER HIS BODY.
CHRIST.
NEARLY HAD THE SAME THING HAPPEN TO ME IN EAST BERLIN.
FIRST THE MESS IN SOFIA, THEN THE LOSS OF THE ODESSA NETWORK, THEN THAT THING IN BORNEO.
ADD IN SMERTIN, LIEBER, AND POOR LINDSAY. BEEN A BAD FEW MONTHS FOR THE FIRM.
METHING'S
THE KGB ON
E MOVE--
DREET DREET
MINDER TWO--
--SORRY, MINDER ONE...
...YES, SIR...RIGHT AWAY...
WATSON WANTS US IN THE OPS ROOM.

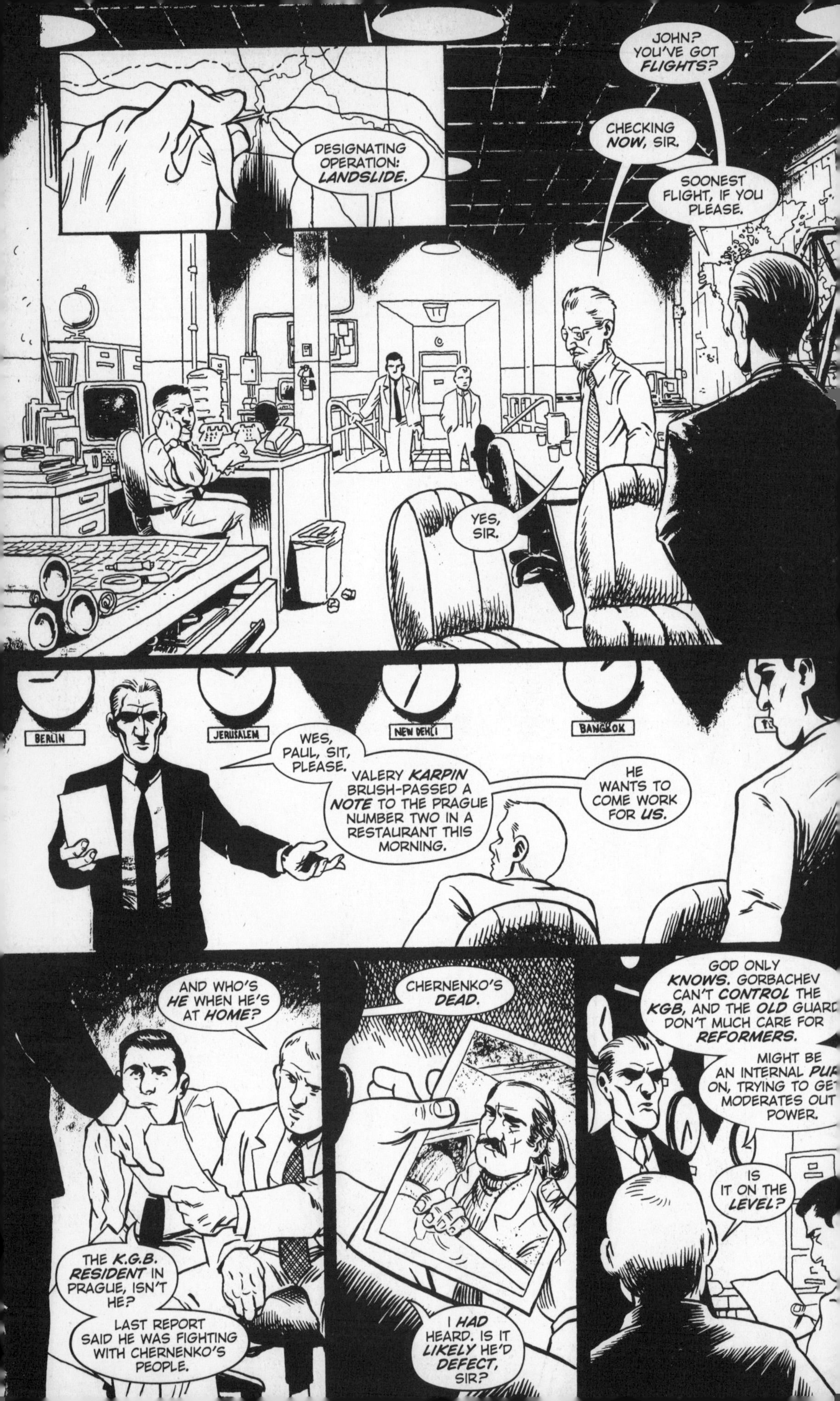
DESIGNATING OPERATION: LANDSLIDE.
JOHN? YOU'VE GOT FLIGHTS?
CHECKING NOW, SIR.
SOONEST FLIGHT, IF YOU PLEASE.
YES, SIR.
BERLIN
JERUSALEM
NEW DEHLI
WES, PAUL, SIT, PLEASE.
VALERY KARPIN BRUSH-PASSED A NOTE TO THE PRAGUE NUMBER TWO IN A RESTAURANT THIS MORNING.
HE WANTS TO COME WORK FOR US.
AND WHO'S HE WHEN HE'S AT HOME?
THE K.G.B. RESIDENT IN PRAGUE, ISN'T HE?
LAST REPORT SAID HE WAS FIGHTING WITH CHERNENKO'S PEOPLE.
CHERNENKO'S DEAD.
I HAD HEARD. IS IT LIKELY HE'D DEFECT, SIR?
GOD ONLY KNOWS. GORBACHEV CAN'T CONTROL THE KGB, AND THE OLD GUARD DON'T MUCH CARE FOR REFORMERS.
MIGHT BE AN INTERNAL PU ON, TRYING TO GET MODERATES OUT POWER.
IS IT ON THE LEVEL?

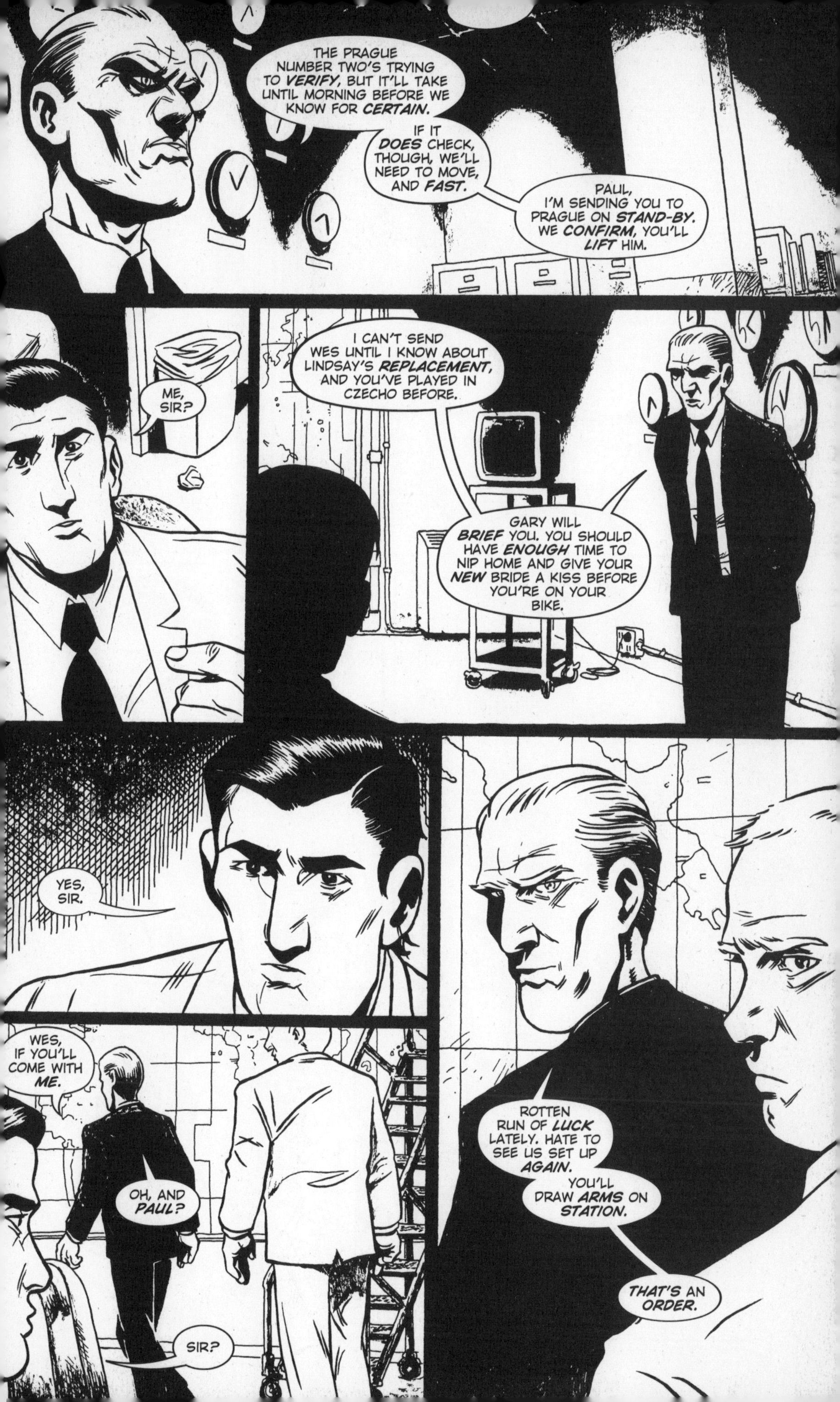
THE PRAGUE NUMBER TWO'S TRYING TO VERIFY, BUT IT'LL TAKE UNTIL MORNING BEFORE WE KNOW FOR CERTAIN.
IF IT DOES CHECK, THOUGH, WE'LL NEED TO MOVE, AND FAST.
PAUL, I'M SENDING YOU TO PRAGUE ON STAND-BY. WE CONFIRM, YOU'LL LIFT HIM.
ME, SIR?
I CAN'T SEND WES UNTIL I KNOW ABOUT LINDSAY'S REPLACEMENT, AND YOU'VE PLAYED IN CZECHO BEFORE.
GARY WILL BRIEF YOU. YOU SHOULD HAVE ENOUGH TIME TO NIP HOME AND GIVE YOUR NEW BRIDE A KISS BEFORE YOU'RE ON YOUR BIKE.
YES, SIR.
WES, IF YOU'LL COME WITH ME.
OH, AND PAUL?
SIR?
ROTTEN RUN OF LUCK LATELY. HATE TO SEE US SET UP AGAIN.
YOU'LL DRAW ARMS ON STATION.
THAT'S AN ORDER.

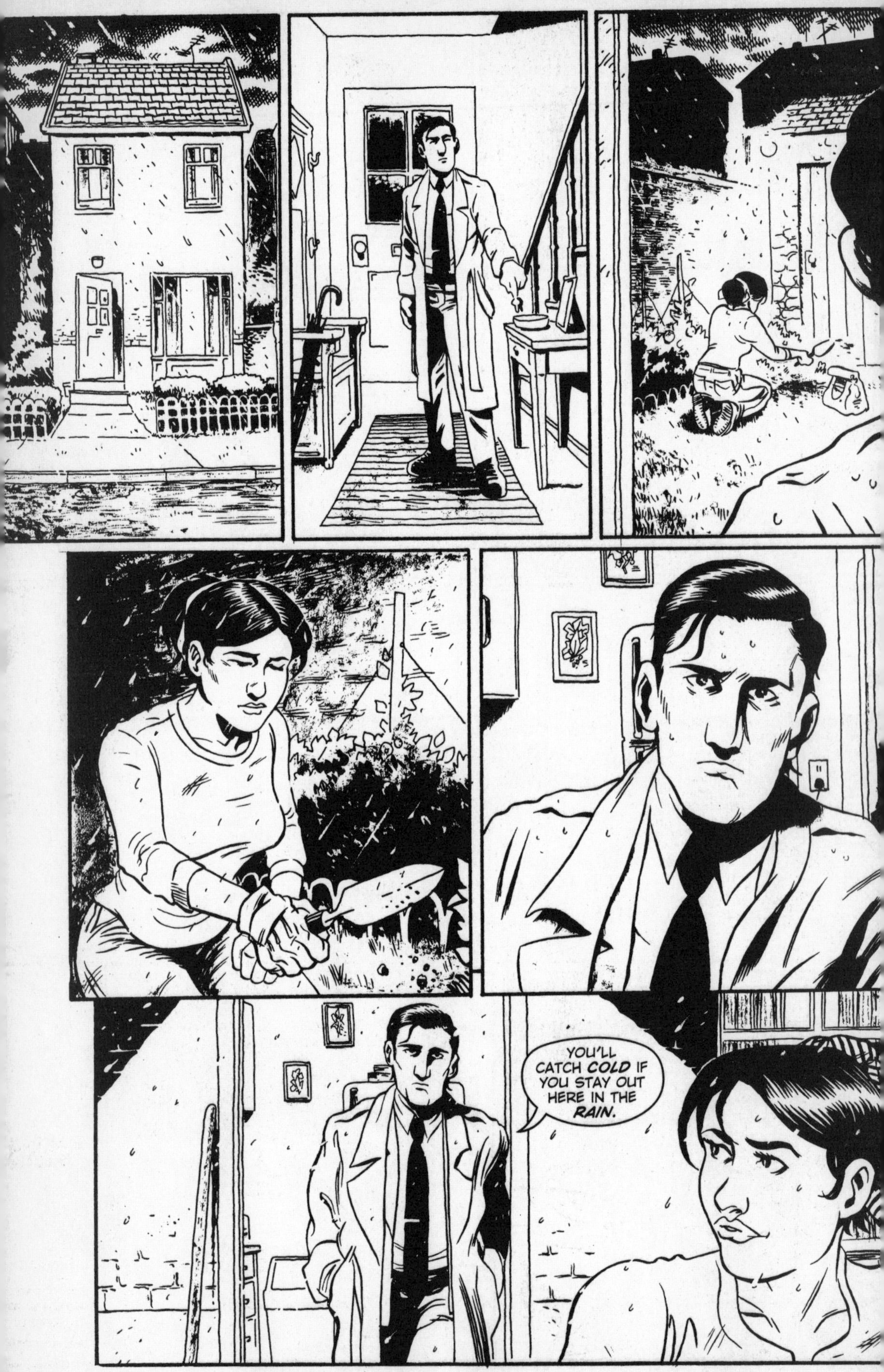
YOU'LL CATCH COLD IF YOU STAY OUT HERE IN THE RAIN.

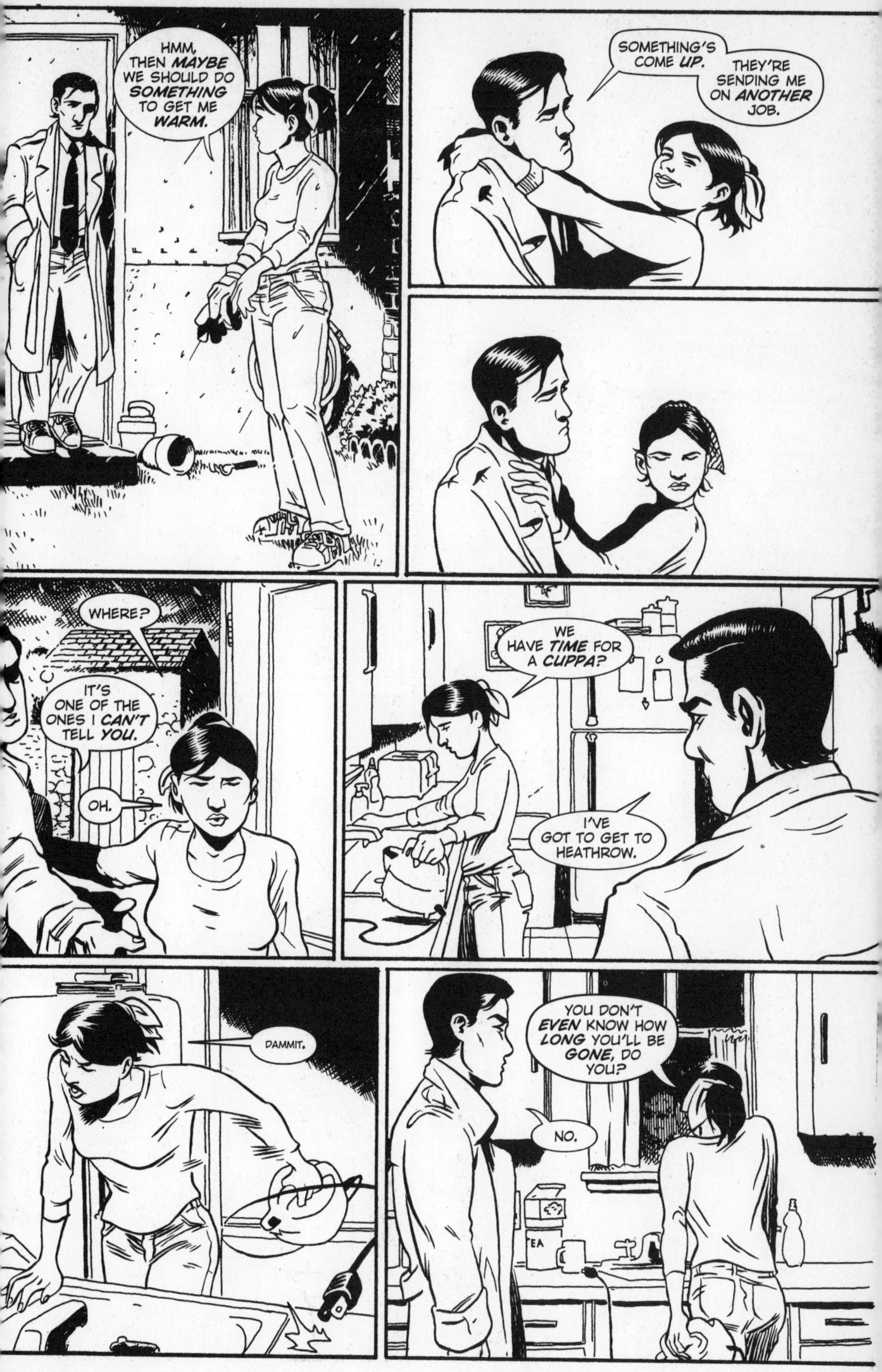
HMM, THEN MAYBE WE SHOULD DO SOMETHING TO GET ME WARM.
SOMETHING'S COME UP.
THEY'RE SENDING ME ON ANOTHER JOB.
WHERE?
IT'S ONE OF THE ONES I CAN'T TELL YOU.
OH.
WE HAVE TIME FOR A CUPPA?
I'VE GOT TO GET TO HEATHROW.
DAMMIT.
YOU DON'T EVEN KNOW HOW LONG YOU'LL BE GONE, DO YOU?
NO.
TEA

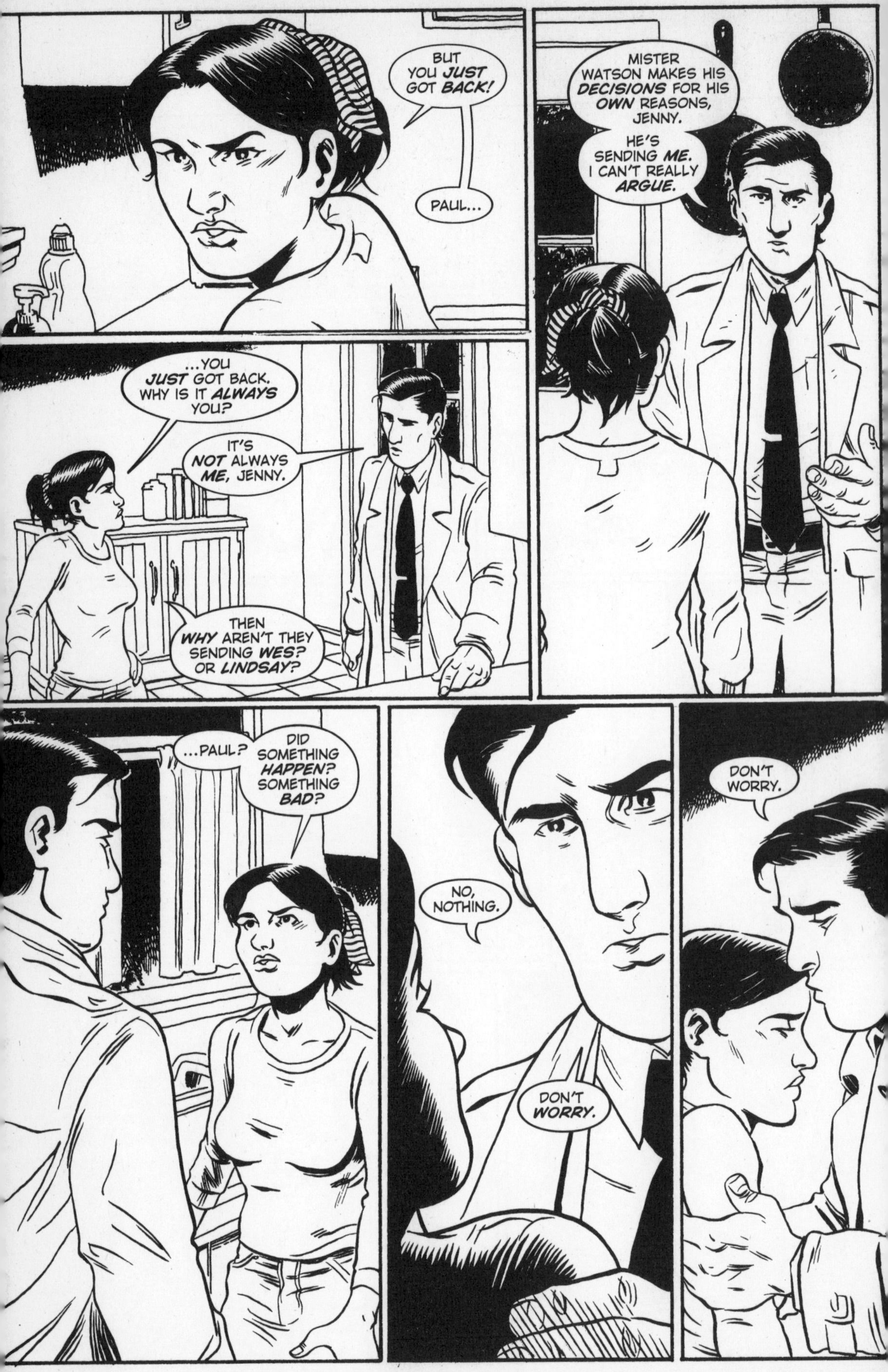
BUT YOU JUST GOT BACK!
PAUL...
MISTER WATSON MAKES HIS DECISIONS FOR HIS OWN REASONS, JENNY.
HE'S SENDING ME. I CAN'T REALLY ARGUE.
...YOU JUST GOT BACK. WHY IS IT ALWAYS YOU?
IT'S NOT ALWAYS ME, JENNY.
THEN WHY AREN'T THEY SENDING WES? OR LINDSAY?
...PAUL?
DID SOMETHING HAPPEN? SOMETHING BAD?
NO, NOTHING.
DON'T WORRY.
DON'T WORRY.

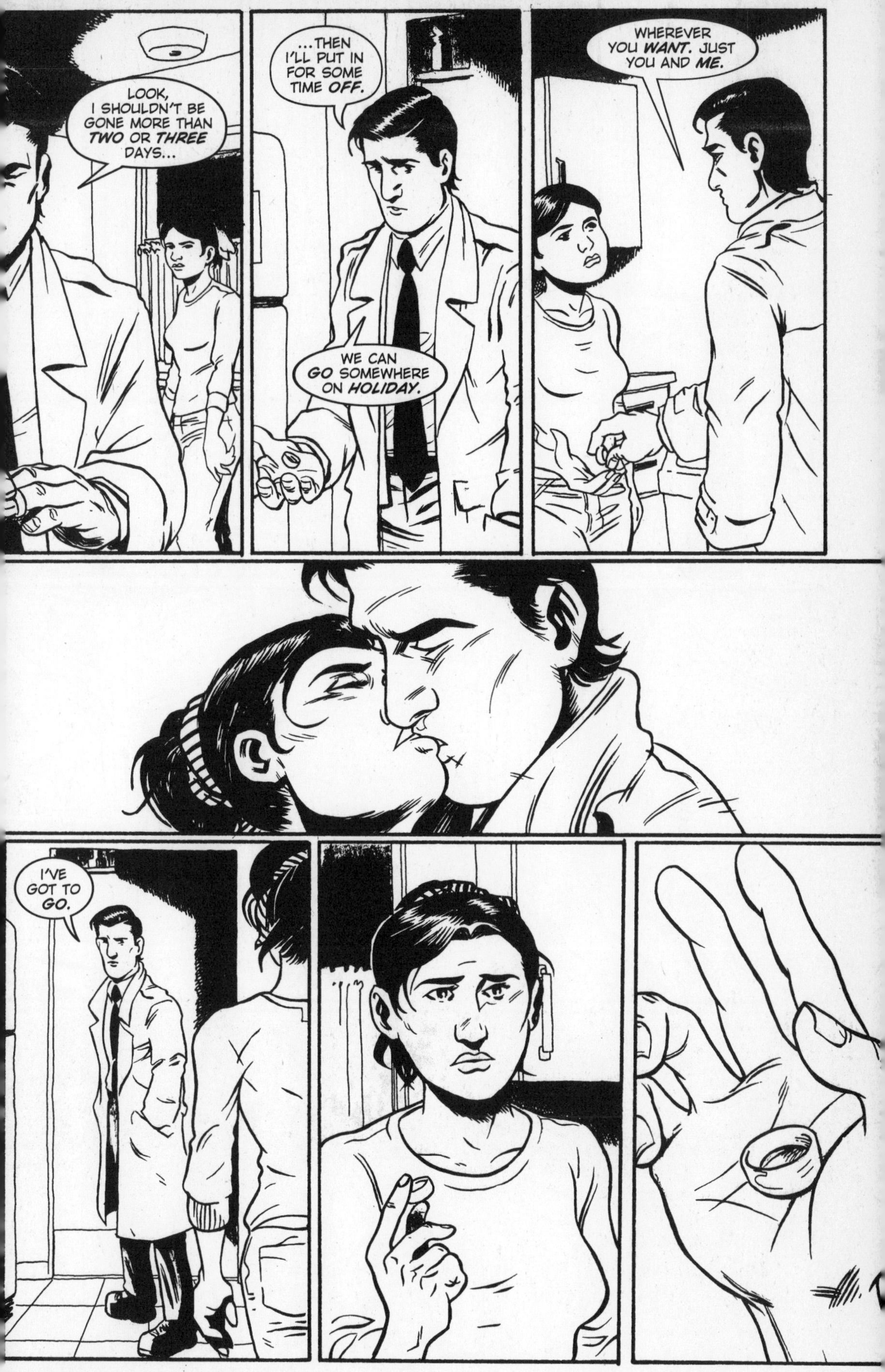

LOOK, I SHOULDN'T BE GONE MORE THAN TWO OR THREE DAYS...
...THEN I'LL PUT IN FOR SOME TIME OFF.
WE CAN GO SOMEWHERE ON HOLIDAY.
WHEREVER YOU WANT. JUST YOU AND ME.
I'VE GOT TO GO.

CHAPTER 2

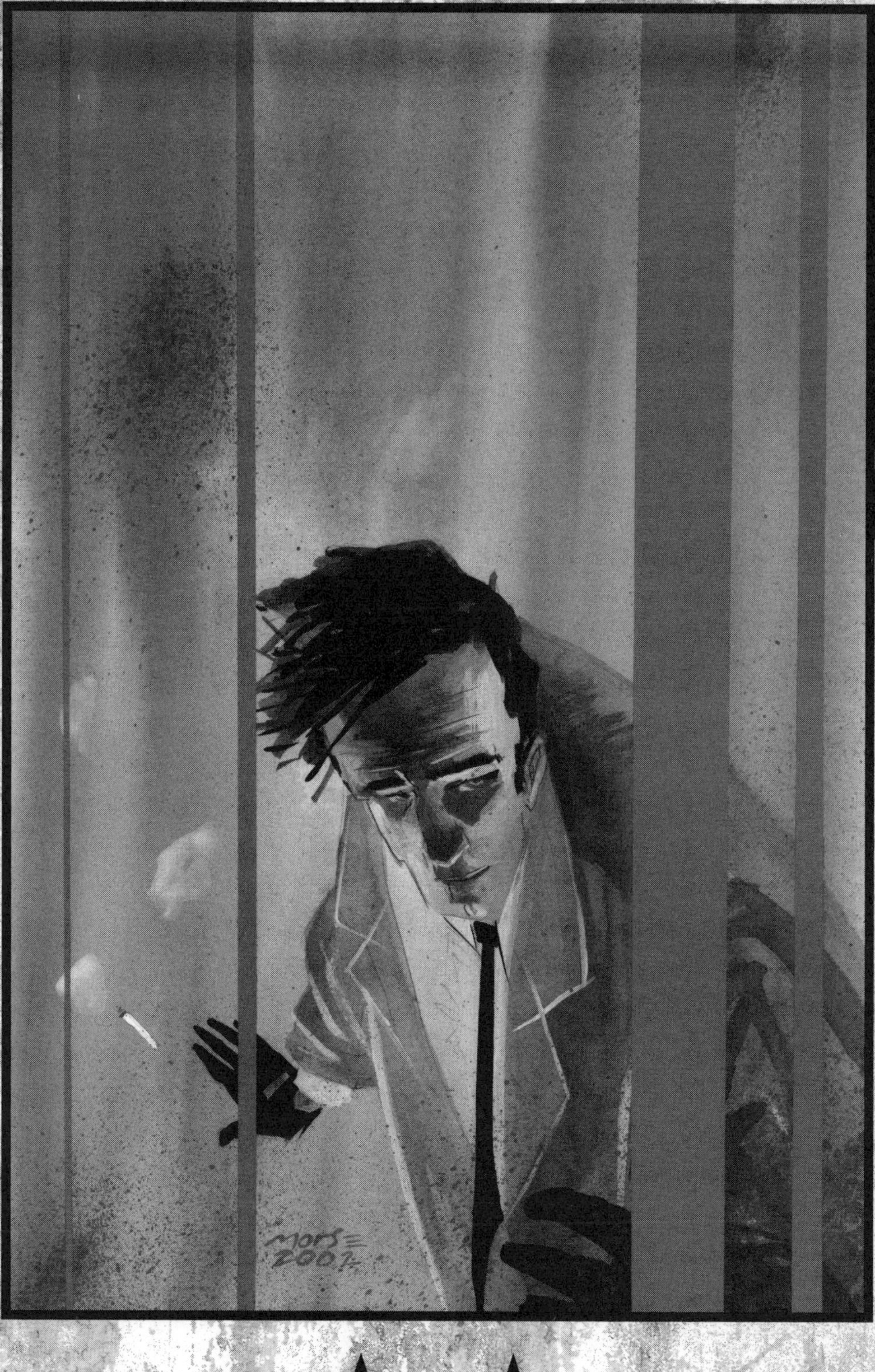

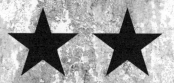

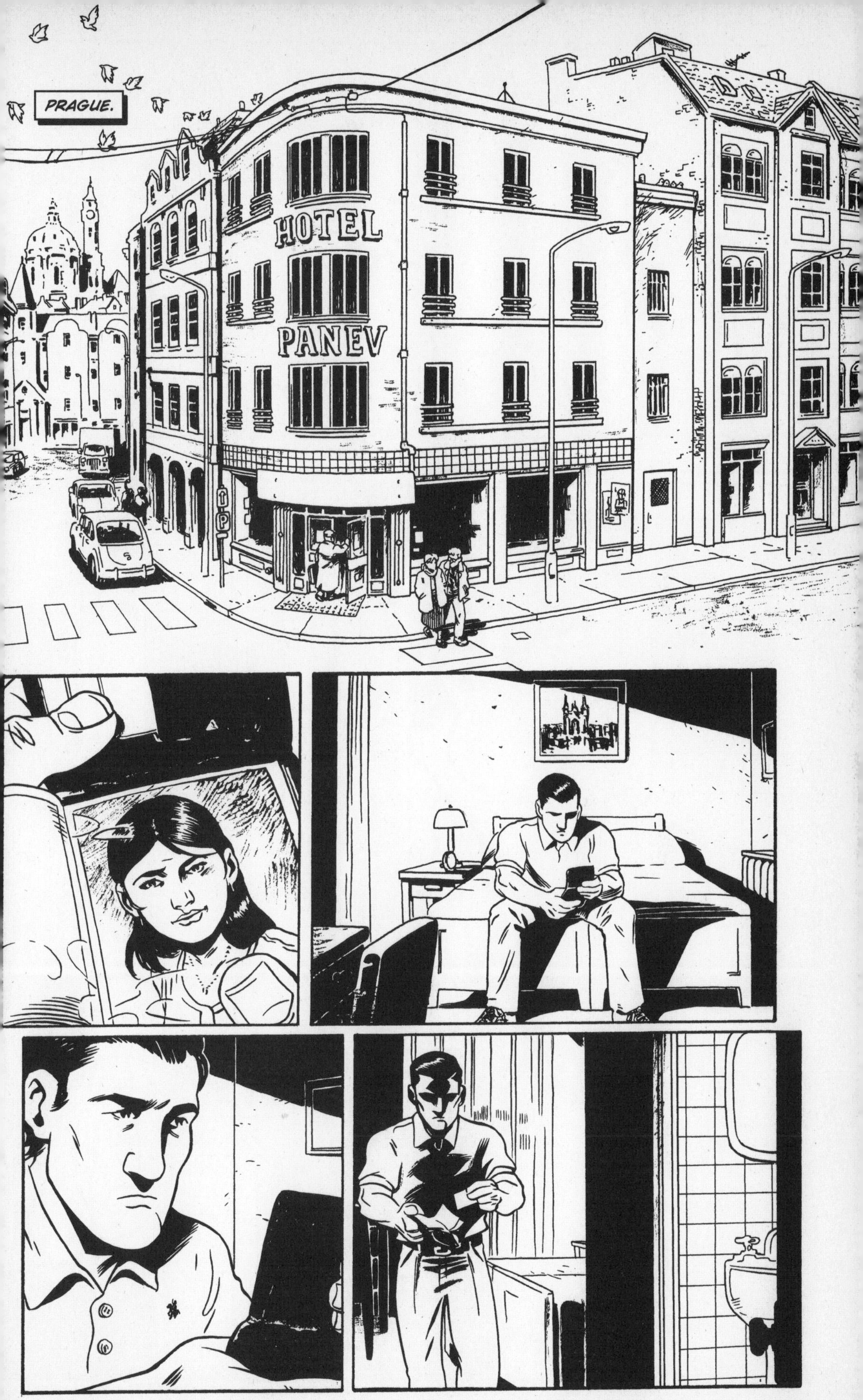
PRAGUE.
HOTEL
PANEV

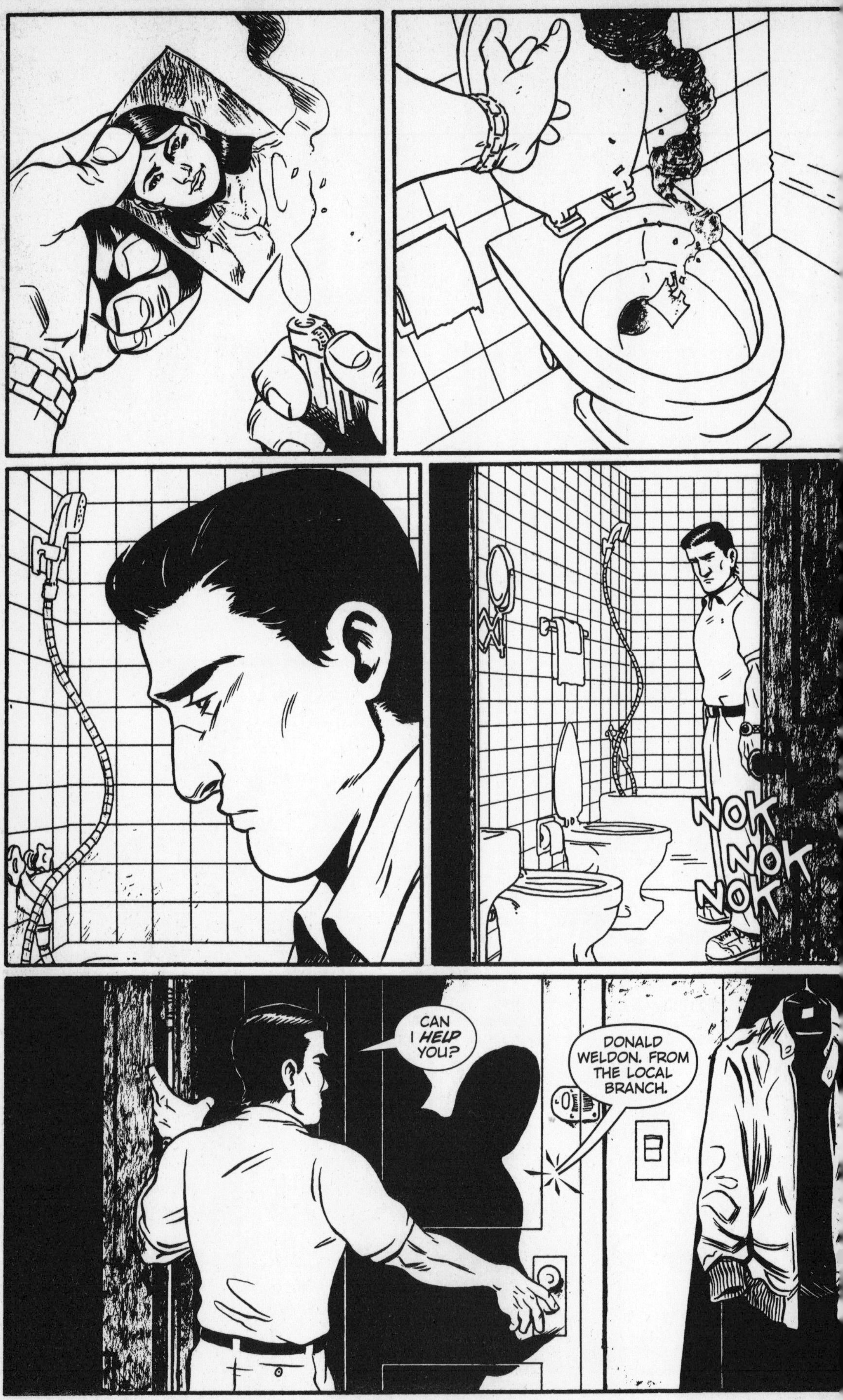
NOK
NOK
NOK
CAN I HELP YOU?
DONALD WELDON. FROM THE LOCAL BRANCH.

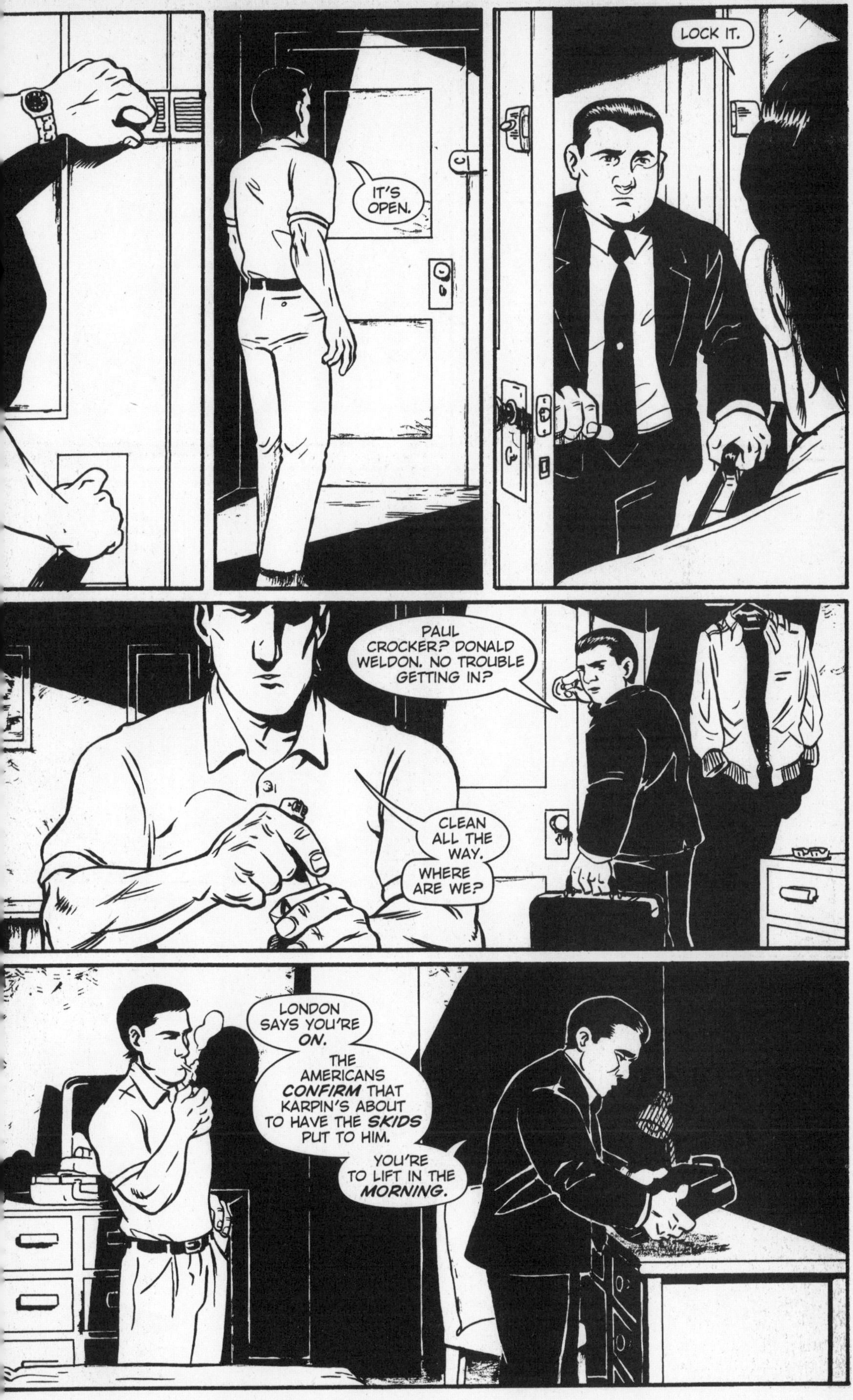
IT'S OPEN.
LOCK IT.
PAUL CROCKER? DONALD WELDON. NO TROUBLE GETTING IN?
CLEAN ALL THE WAY.
WHERE ARE WE?
LONDON SAYS YOU'RE ON.
THE AMERICANS CONFIRM THAT KARPIN'S ABOUT TO HAVE THE SKIDS PUT TO HIM.
YOU'RE TO LIFT IN THE MORNING.

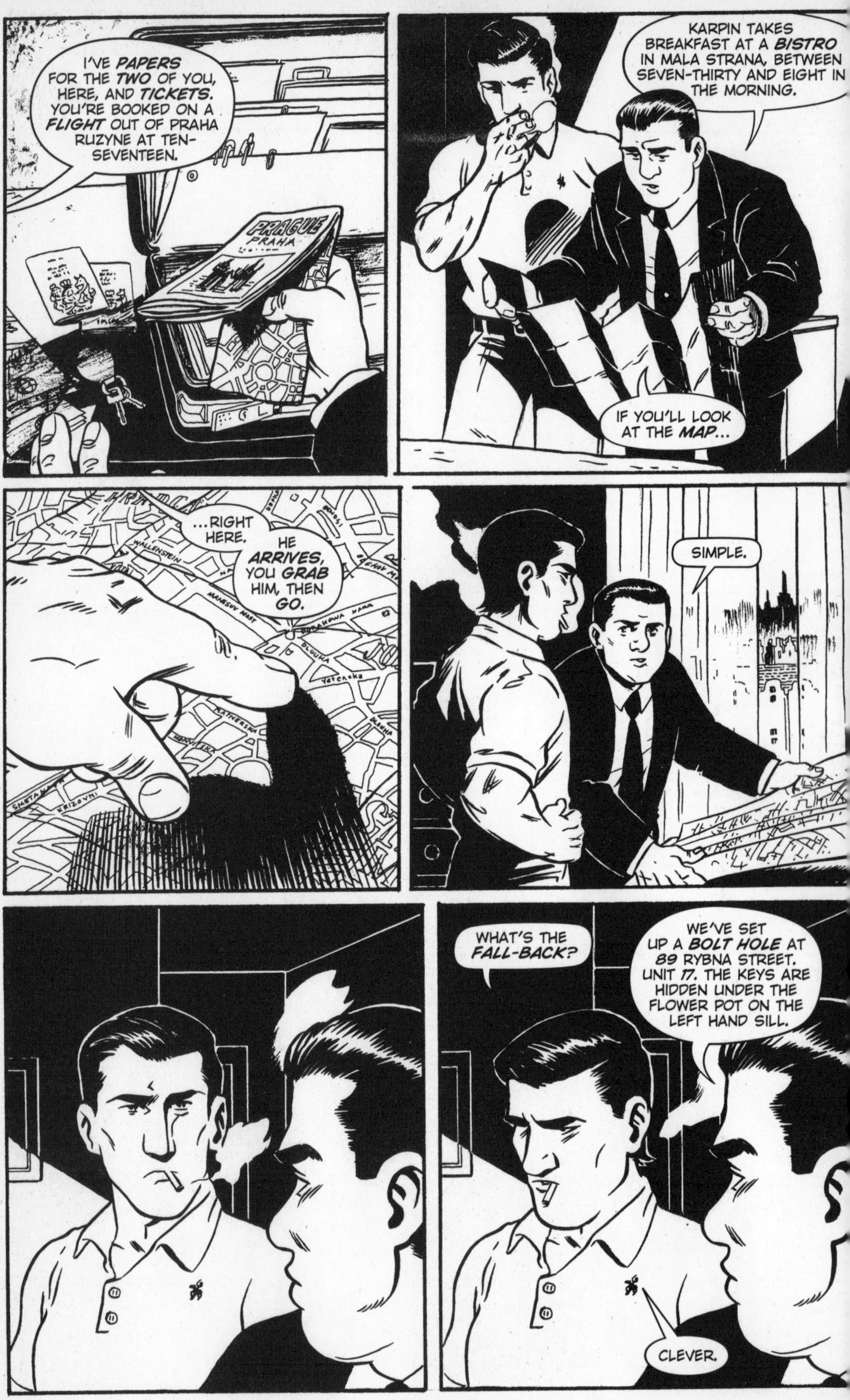
I'VE PAPERS FOR THE TWO OF YOU, HERE, AND TICKETS. YOU'RE BOOKED ON A FLIGHT OUT OF PRAHA RUZYNE AT TEN-SEVENTEEN.
PRAGUE
PRAHA
KARPIN TAKES BREAKFAST AT A BISTRO IN MALA STRANA, BETWEEN SEVEN-THIRTY AND EIGHT IN THE MORNING.
IF YOU'LL LOOK AT THE MAP...
...RIGHT HERE.
HE ARRIVES, YOU GRAB HIM, THEN GO.
SIMPLE.
WHAT'S THE FALL-BACK?
WE'VE SET UP A BOLT HOLE AT 89 RYBNA STREET. UNIT 17. THE KEYS ARE HIDDEN UNDER THE FLOWER POT ON THE LEFT HAND SILL.
CLEVER.

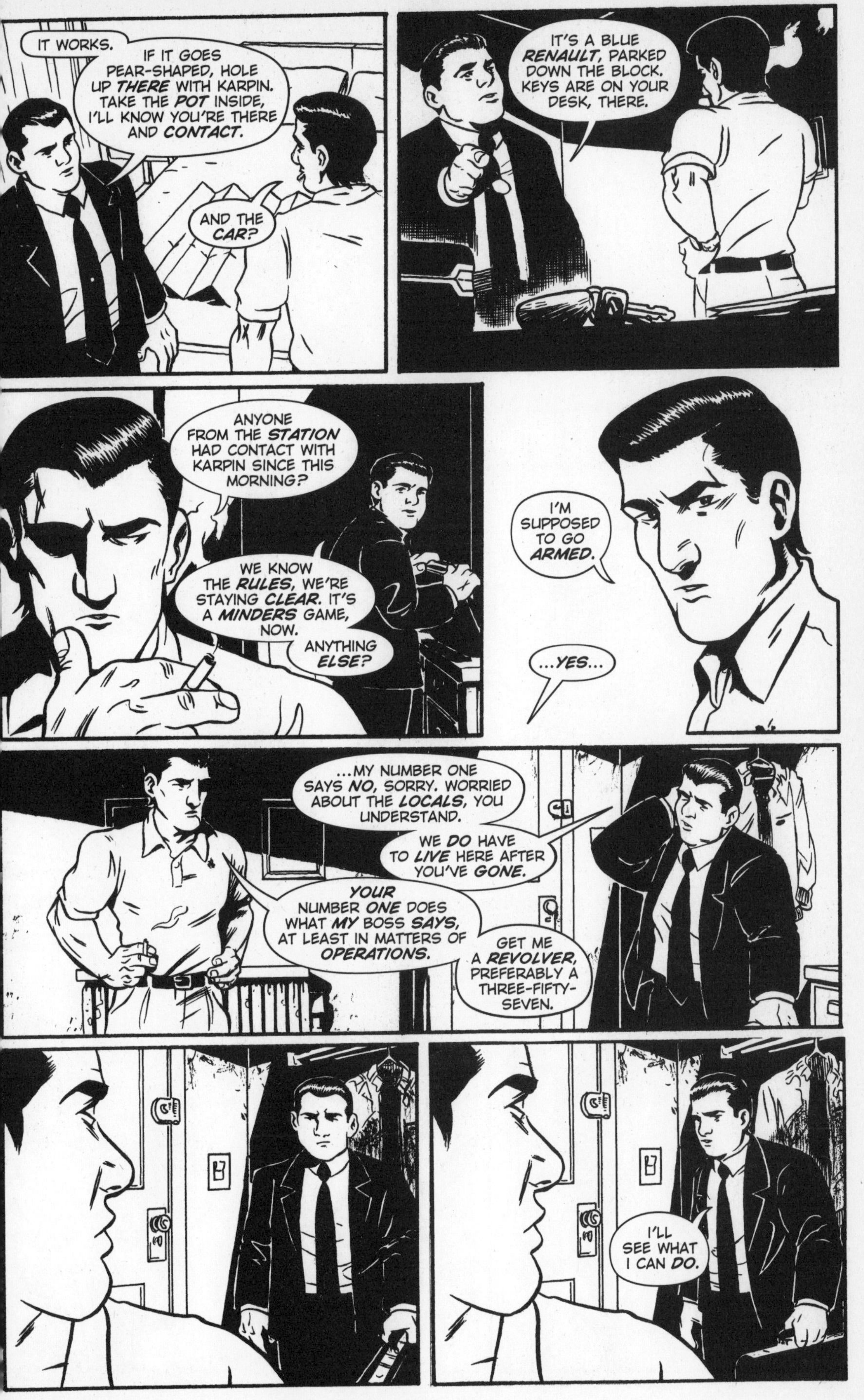
IT WORKS.
IF IT GOES PEAR-SHAPED, HOLE UP THERE WITH KARPIN. TAKE THE POT INSIDE, I'LL KNOW YOU'RE THERE AND CONTACT.
AND THE CAR?
IT'S A BLUE RENAULT, PARKED DOWN THE BLOCK. KEYS ARE ON YOUR DESK, THERE.
ANYONE FROM THE STATION HAD CONTACT WITH KARPIN SINCE THIS MORNING?
WE KNOW THE RULES, WE'RE STAYING CLEAR. IT'S A MINDERS GAME, NOW.
ANYTHING ELSE?
I'M SUPPOSED TO GO ARMED.
...YES...
...MY NUMBER ONE SAYS NO, SORRY. WORRIED ABOUT THE LOCALS, YOU UNDERSTAND.
WE DO HAVE TO LIVE HERE AFTER YOU'VE GONE.
YOUR NUMBER ONE DOES WHAT MY BOSS SAYS, AT LEAST IN MATTERS OF OPERATIONS.
GET ME A REVOLVER, PREFERABLY A THREE-FIFTY-SEVEN.
I'LL SEE WHAT I CAN DO.

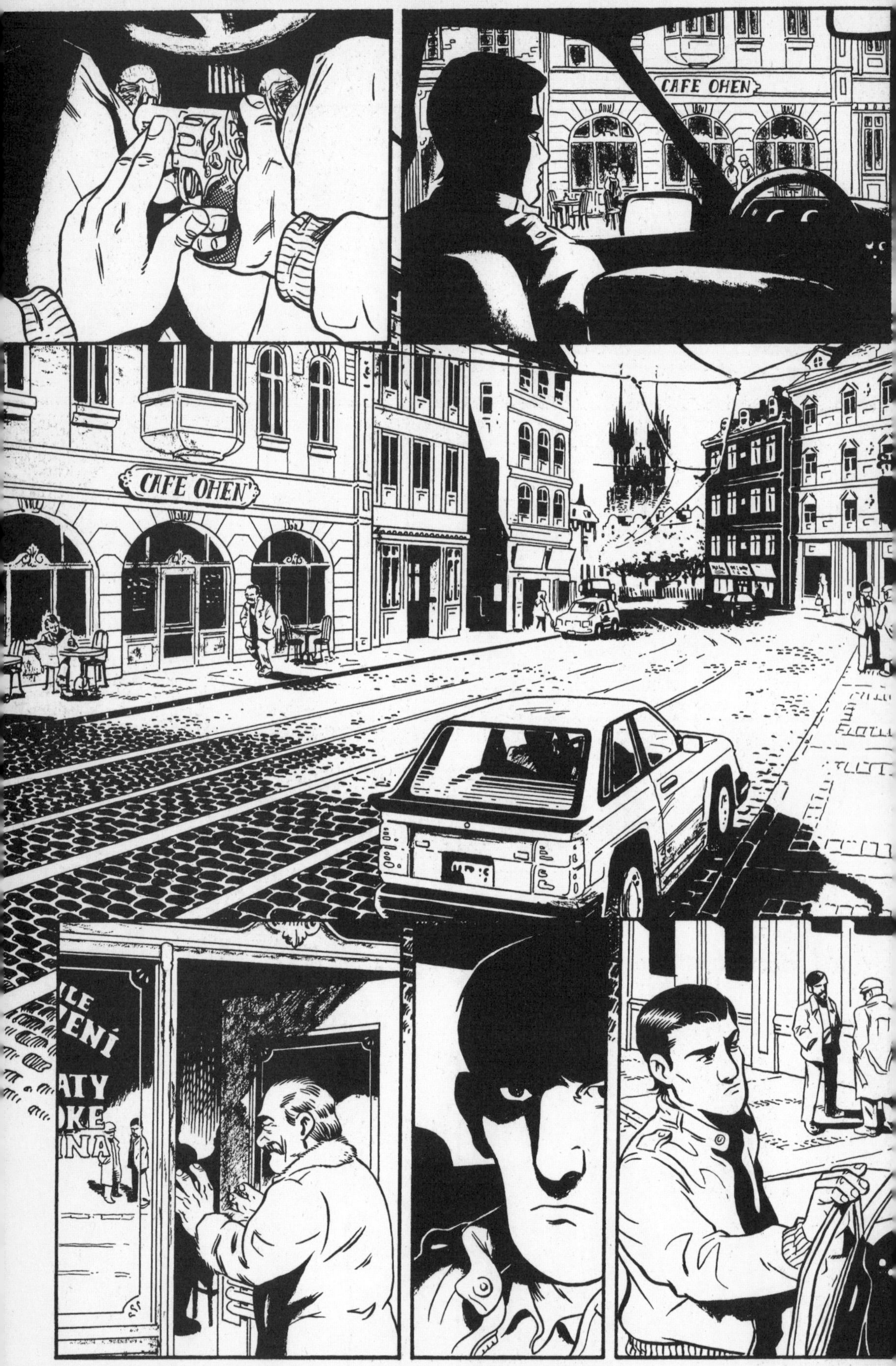
CAFE OHEN
CAFE OHEN

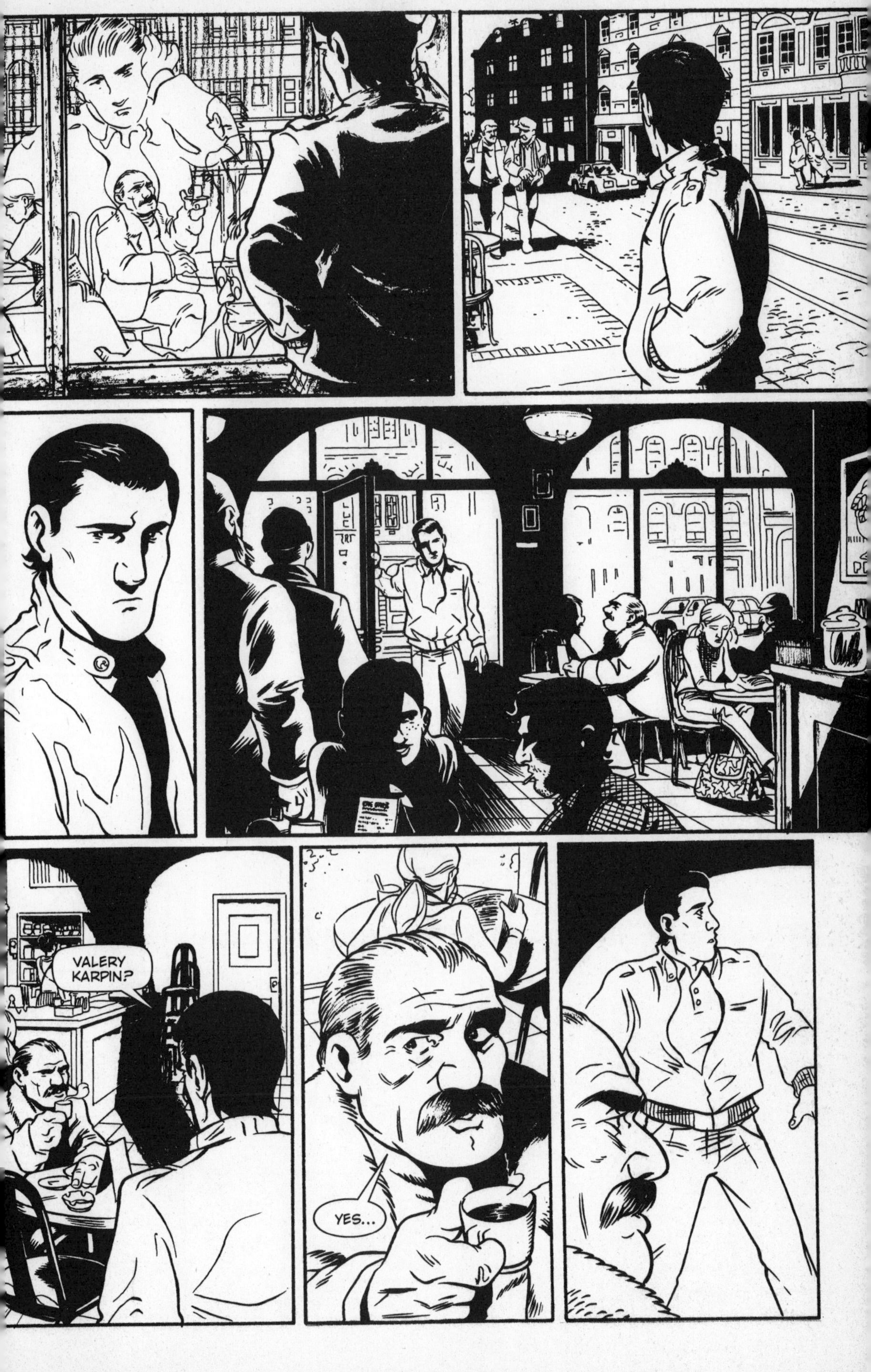
VALERY KARPIN?
YES...

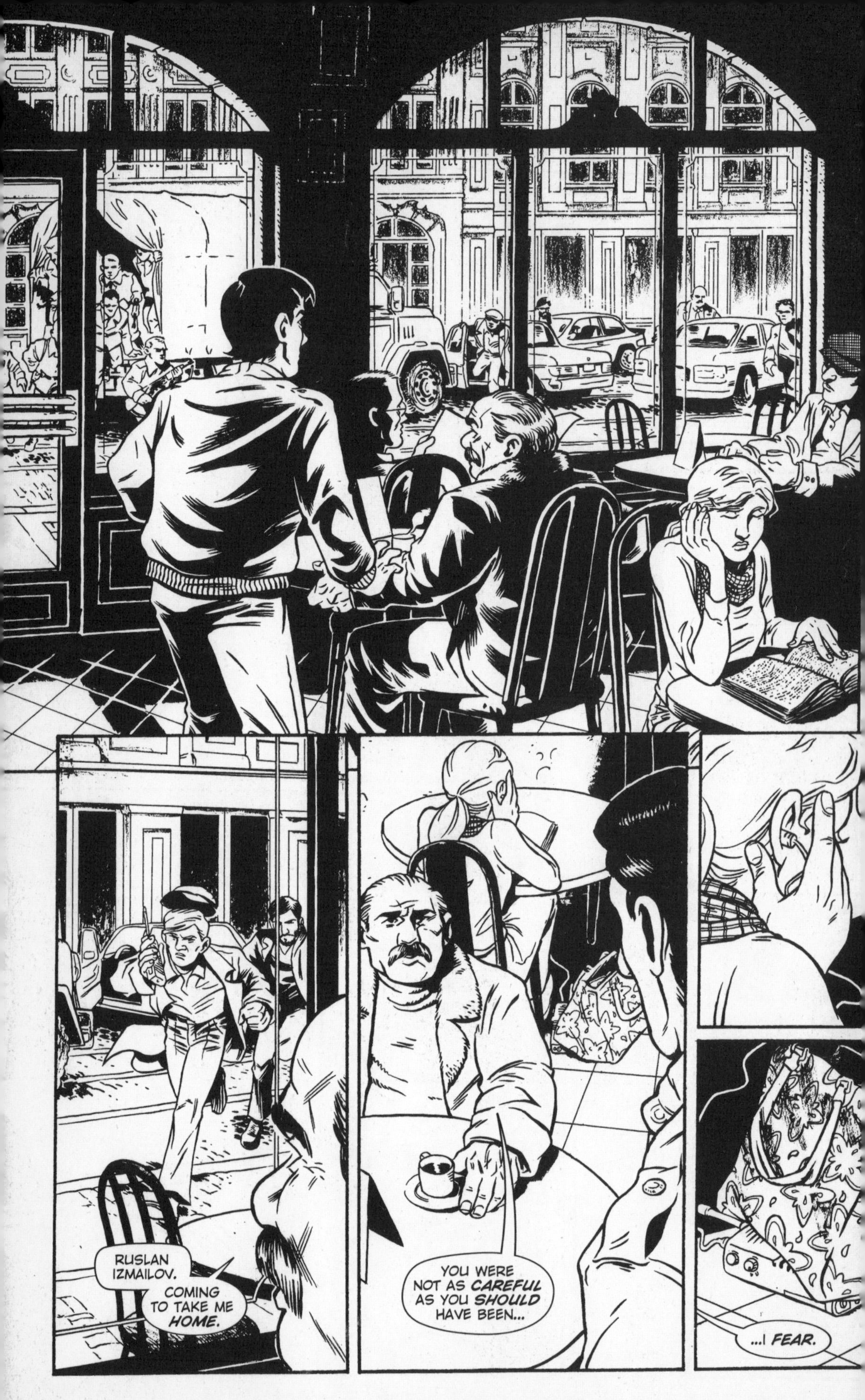
RUSLAN IZMAILOV.
COMING TO TAKE ME HOME.
YOU WERE NOT AS CAREFUL AS YOU SHOULD HAVE BEEN...
...I FEAR.

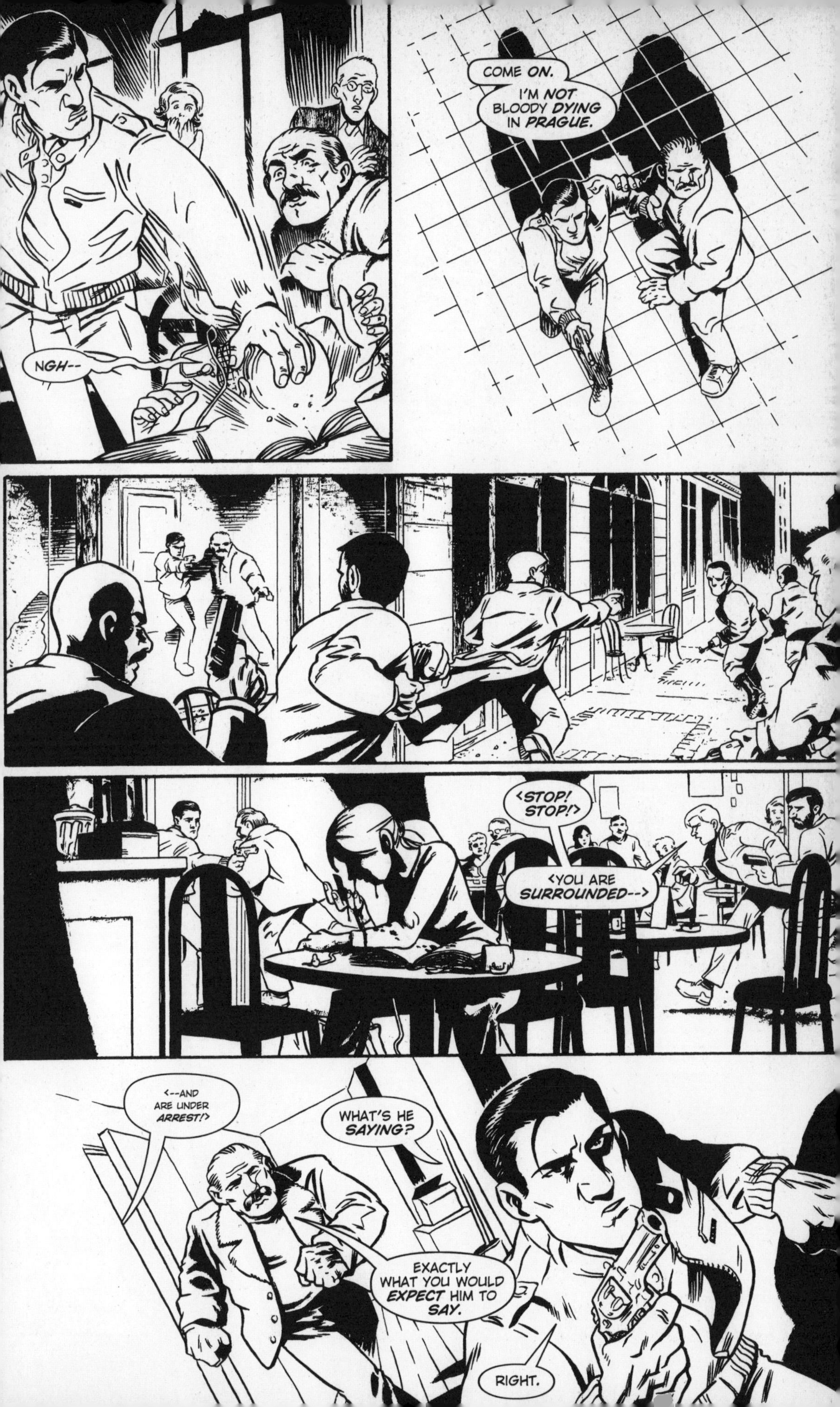
NGH--
COME ON.
I'M NOT BLOODY DYING IN PRAGUE.
<STOP! STOP!>
<YOU ARE SURROUNDED-->
<--AND ARE UNDER ARREST!>
WHAT'S HE SAYING?
EXACTLY WHAT YOU WOULD EXPECT HIM TO SAY.
RIGHT.

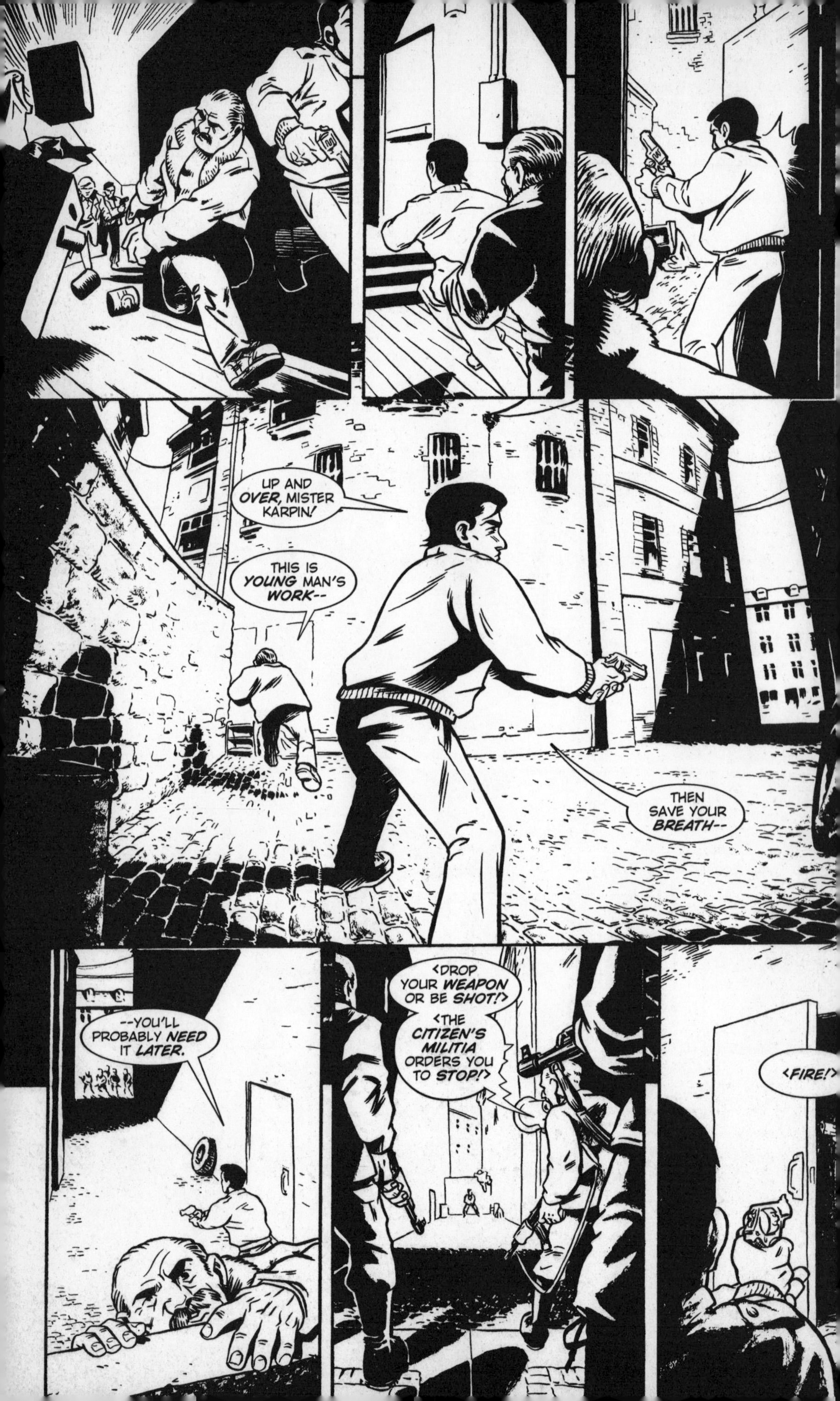
UP AND OVER, MISTER KARPIN!
THIS IS YOUNG MAN'S WORK--
THEN SAVE YOUR BREATH--
--YOU'LL PROBABLY NEED IT LATER.
<DROP YOUR WEAPON OR BE SHOT!>
<THE CITIZEN'S MILITIA ORDERS YOU TO STOP!>
<FIRE!>

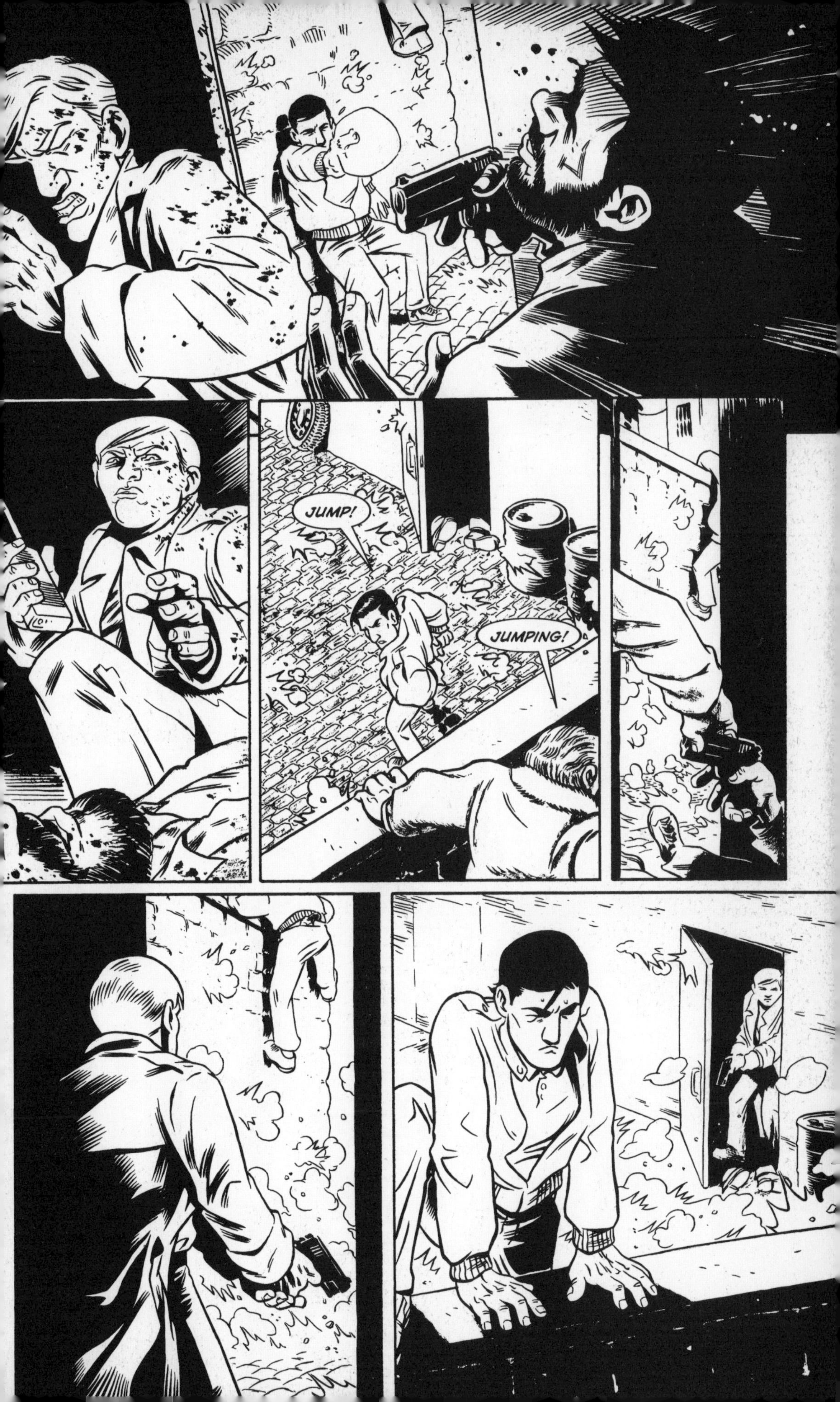
JUMP!
JUMPING!

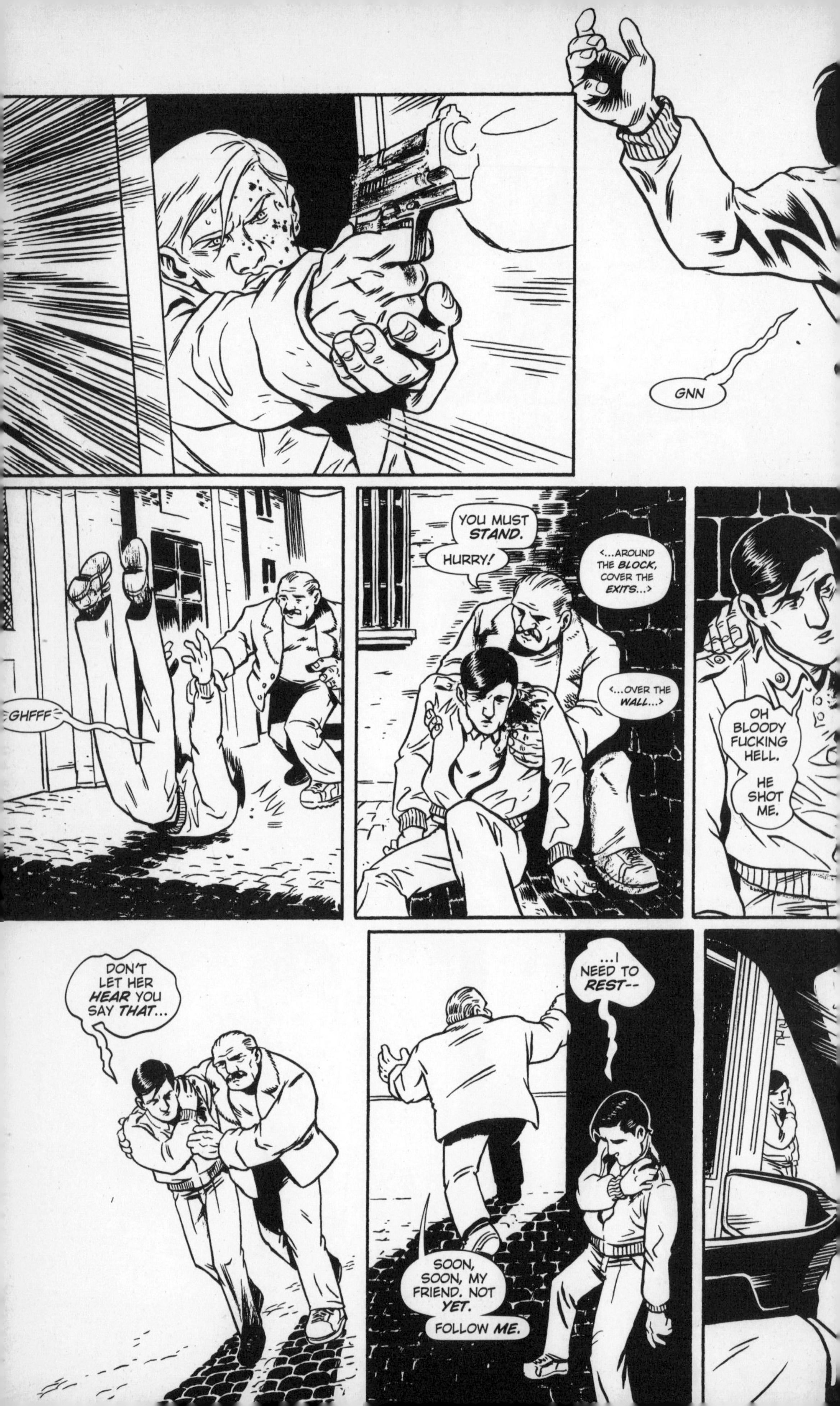
GNN
GHFFF
YOU MUST STAND.
HURRY!
<...AROUND THE BLOCK, COVER THE EXITS...>
<...OVER THE WALL...>
OH BLOODY FUCKING HELL.
HE SHOT ME.
DON'T LET HER HEAR YOU SAY THAT...
...I NEED TO REST--
SOON, SOON, MY FRIEND. NOT YET.
FOLLOW ME.

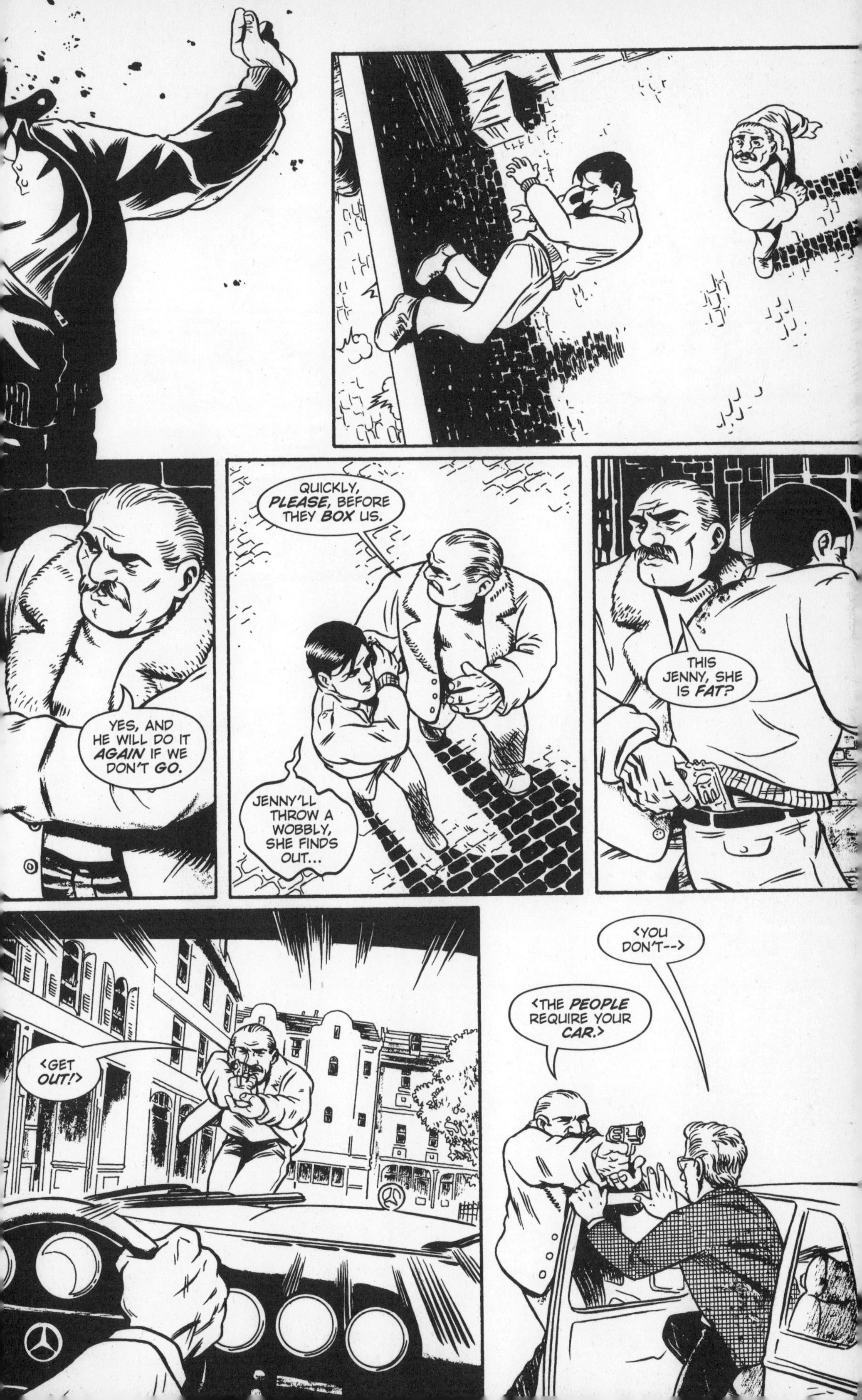
YES, AND HE WILL DO IT AGAIN IF WE DON'T GO.
QUICKLY, PLEASE, BEFORE THEY BOX US.
JENNY'LL THROW A WOBBLY, SHE FINDS OUT...
THIS JENNY, SHE IS FAT?
<GET OUT!>
<YOU DON'T-->
<THE PEOPLE REQUIRE YOUR CAR.>

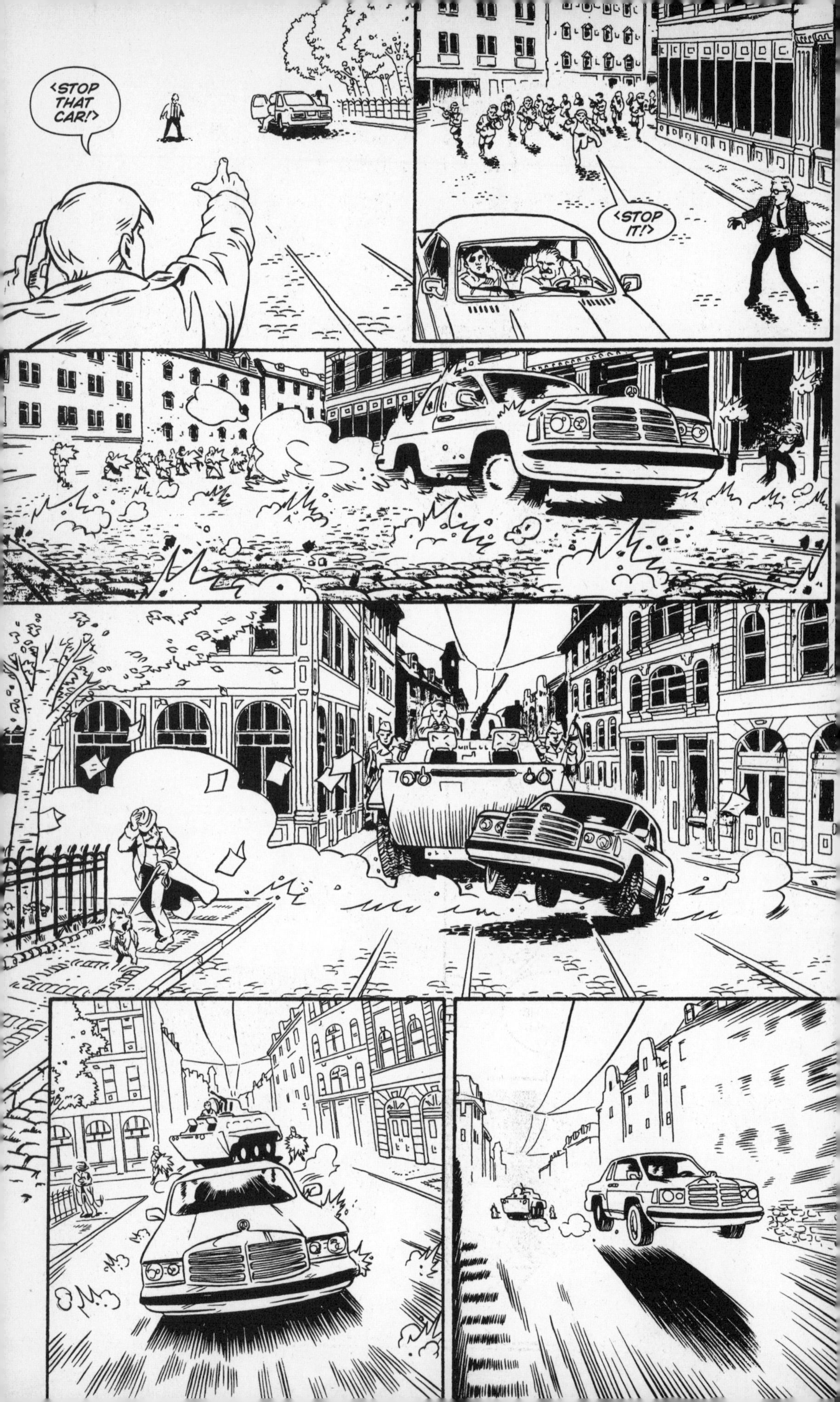
<STOP THAT CAR!>
<STOP IT!>

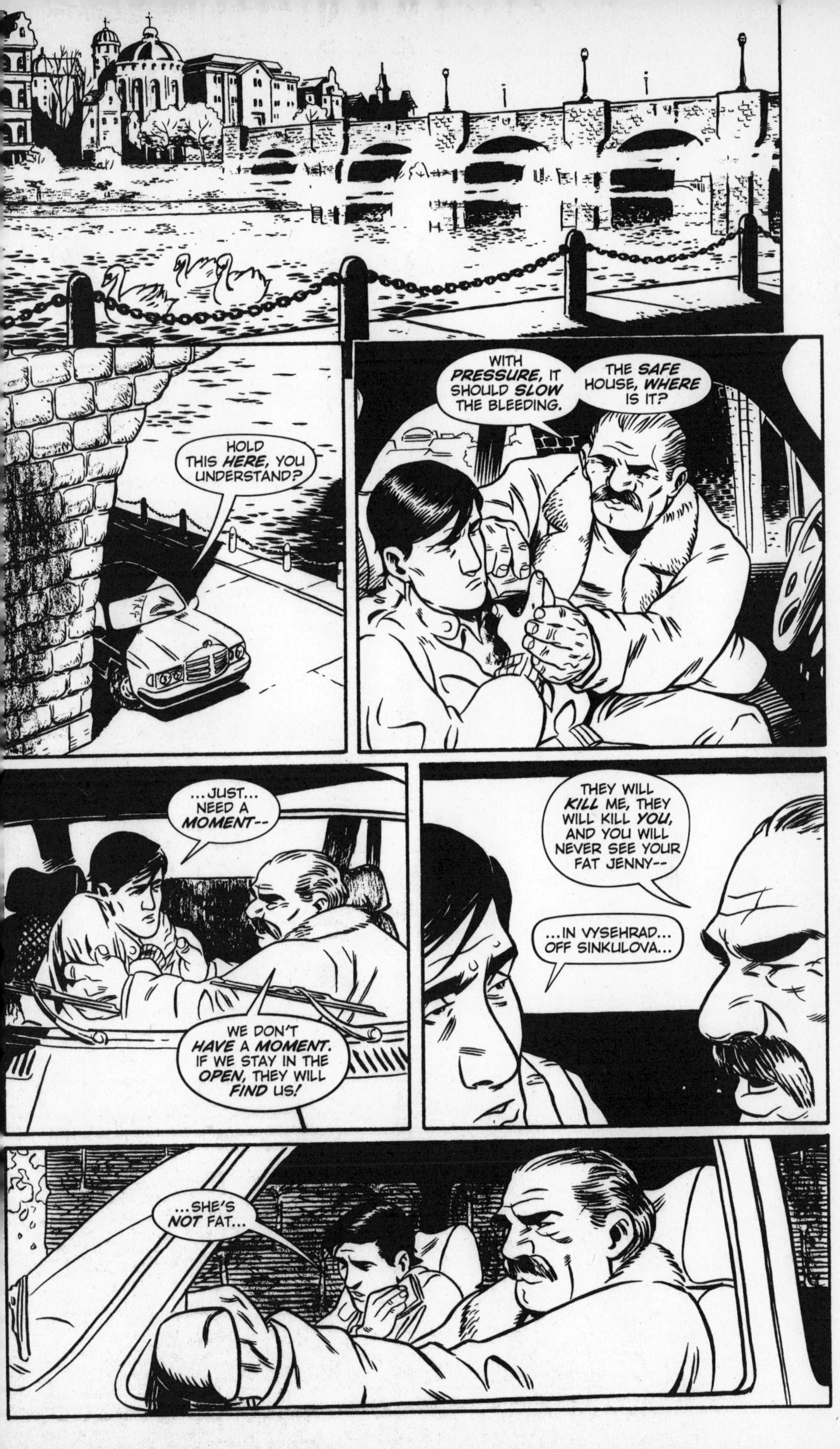
HOLD THIS HERE, YOU UNDERSTAND?
WITH PRESSURE, IT SHOULD SLOW THE BLEEDING.
THE SAFE HOUSE, WHERE IS IT?
...JUST... NEED A MOMENT--
WE DON'T HAVE A MOMENT. IF WE STAY IN THE OPEN, THEY WILL FIND US!
THEY WILL KILL ME, THEY WILL KILL YOU, AND YOU WILL NEVER SEE YOUR FAT JENNY--
...IN VYSEHRAD... OFF SINKULOVA...
...SHE'S NOT FAT...

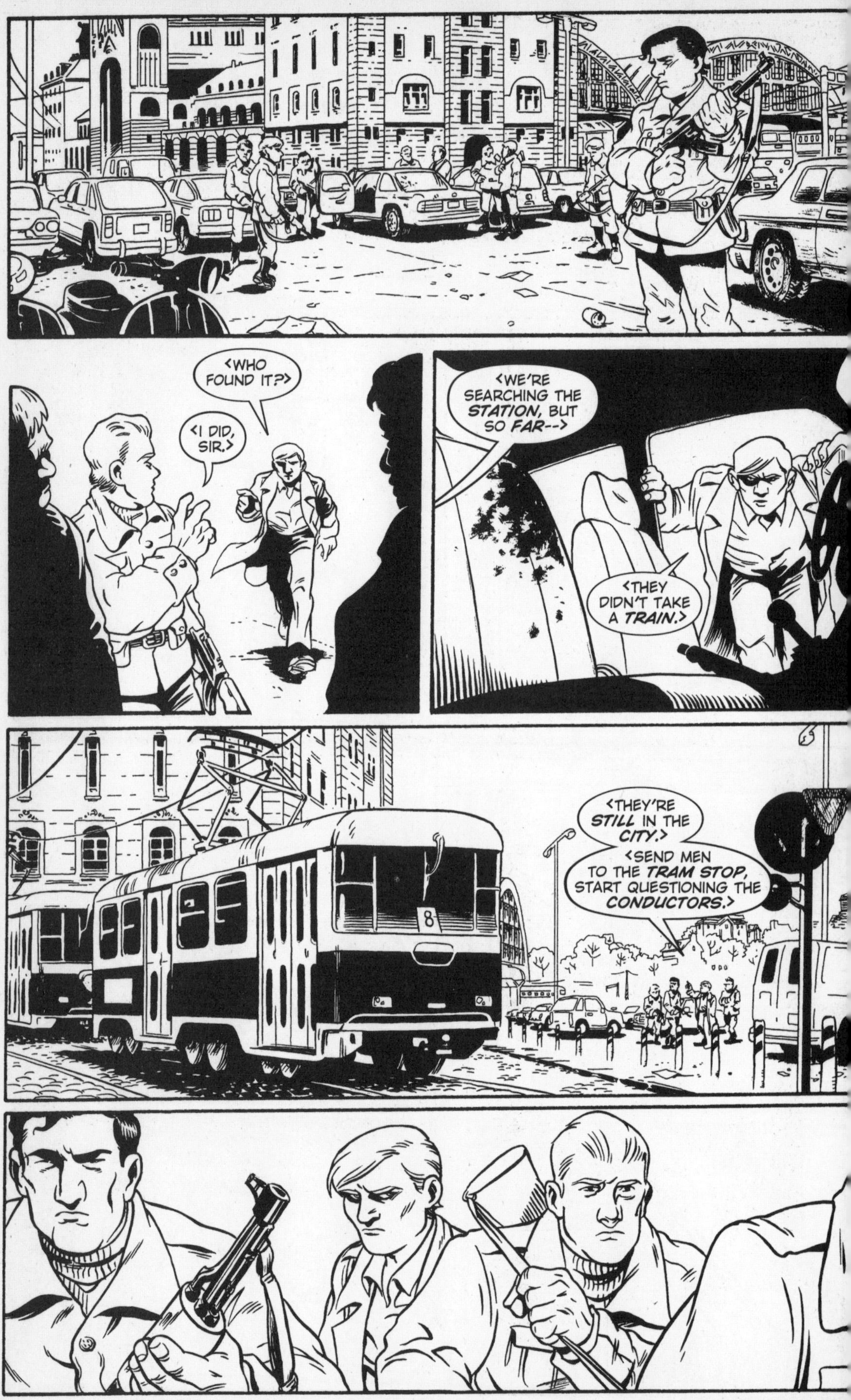
<WHO FOUND IT?>
<I DID, SIR.>
<WE'RE SEARCHING THE STATION, BUT SO FAR-->
<THEY DIDN'T TAKE A TRAIN.>
<THEY'RE STILL IN THE CITY.>
<SEND MEN TO THE TRAM STOP, START QUESTIONING THE CONDUCTORS.>

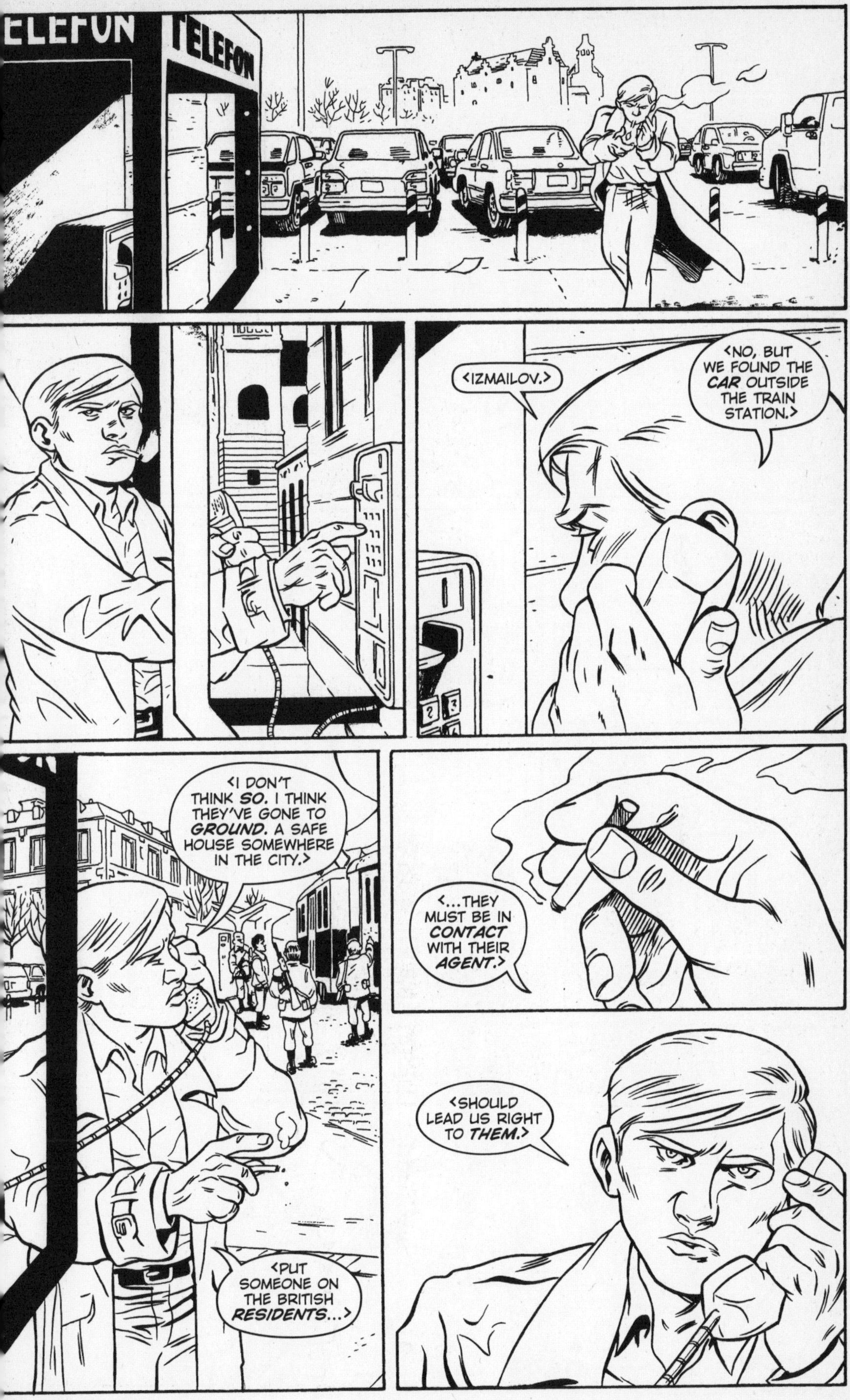
TELEFON
TELEFON
<IZMAILOV.>
<NO, BUT WE FOUND THE CAR OUTSIDE THE TRAIN STATION.>
<I DON'T THINK SO. I THINK THEY'VE GONE TO GROUND. A SAFE HOUSE SOMEWHERE IN THE CITY.>
<PUT SOMEONE ON THE BRITISH RESIDENTS...>
<...THEY MUST BE IN CONTACT WITH THEIR AGENT.>
<SHOULD LEAD US RIGHT TO THEM.>

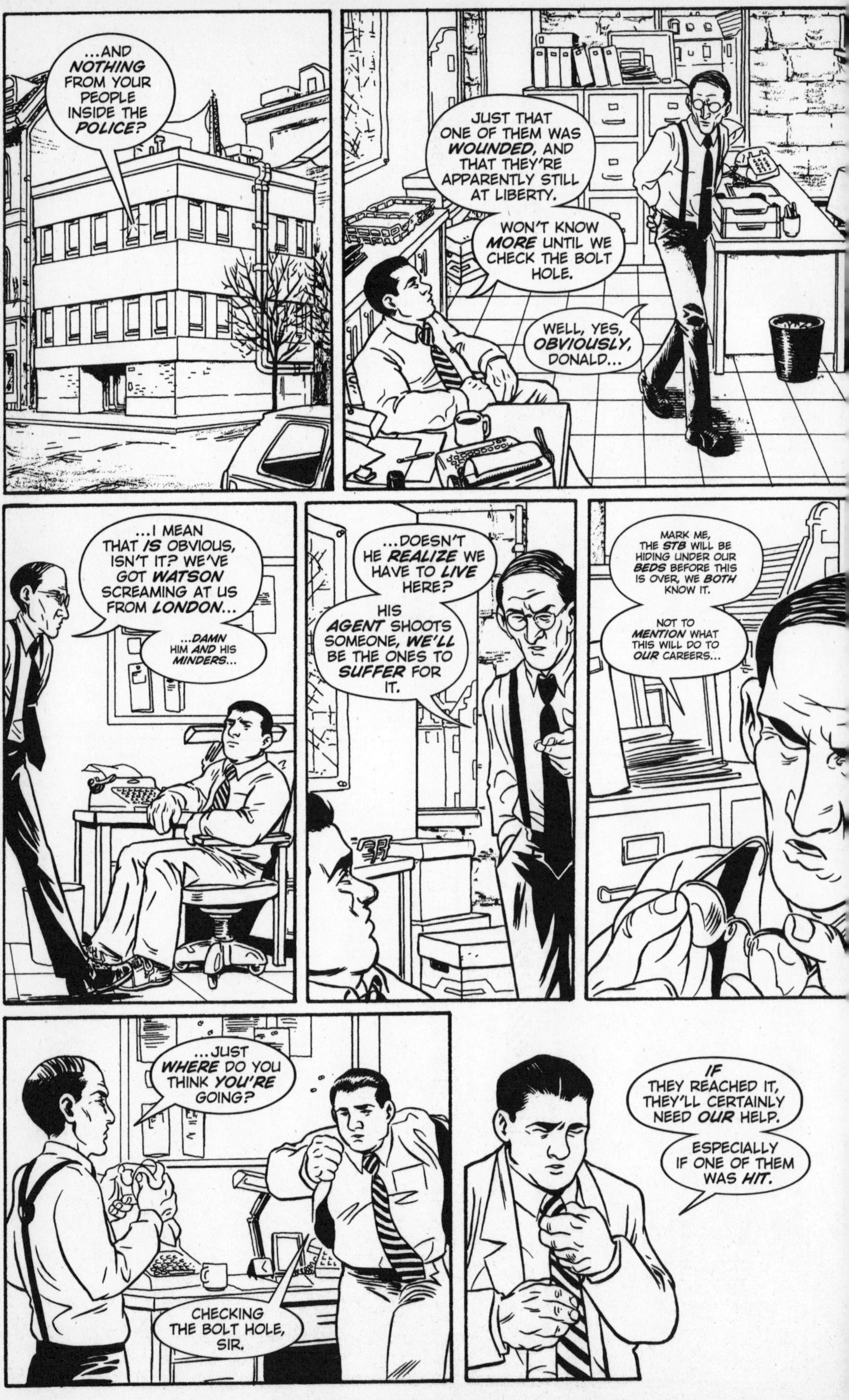
...AND NOTHING FROM YOUR PEOPLE INSIDE THE POLICE?
JUST THAT ONE OF THEM WAS WOUNDED, AND THAT THEY'RE APPARENTLY STILL AT LIBERTY.
WON'T KNOW MORE UNTIL WE CHECK THE BOLT HOLE.
WELL, YES, OBVIOUSLY, DONALD...
...I MEAN THAT IS OBVIOUS, ISN'T IT? WE'VE GOT WATSON SCREAMING AT US FROM LONDON...
...DAMN HIM AND HIS MINDERS...
...DOESN'T HE REALIZE WE HAVE TO LIVE HERE?
HIS AGENT SHOOTS SOMEONE, WE'LL BE THE ONES TO SUFFER FOR IT.
MARK ME, THE STB WILL BE HIDING UNDER OUR BEDS BEFORE THIS IS OVER, WE BOTH KNOW IT.
NOT TO MENTION WHAT THIS WILL DO TO OUR CAREERS...
...JUST WHERE DO YOU THINK YOU'RE GOING?
CHECKING THE BOLT HOLE, SIR.
IF THEY REACHED IT, THEY'LL CERTAINLY NEED OUR HELP.
ESPECIALLY IF ONE OF THEM WAS HIT.

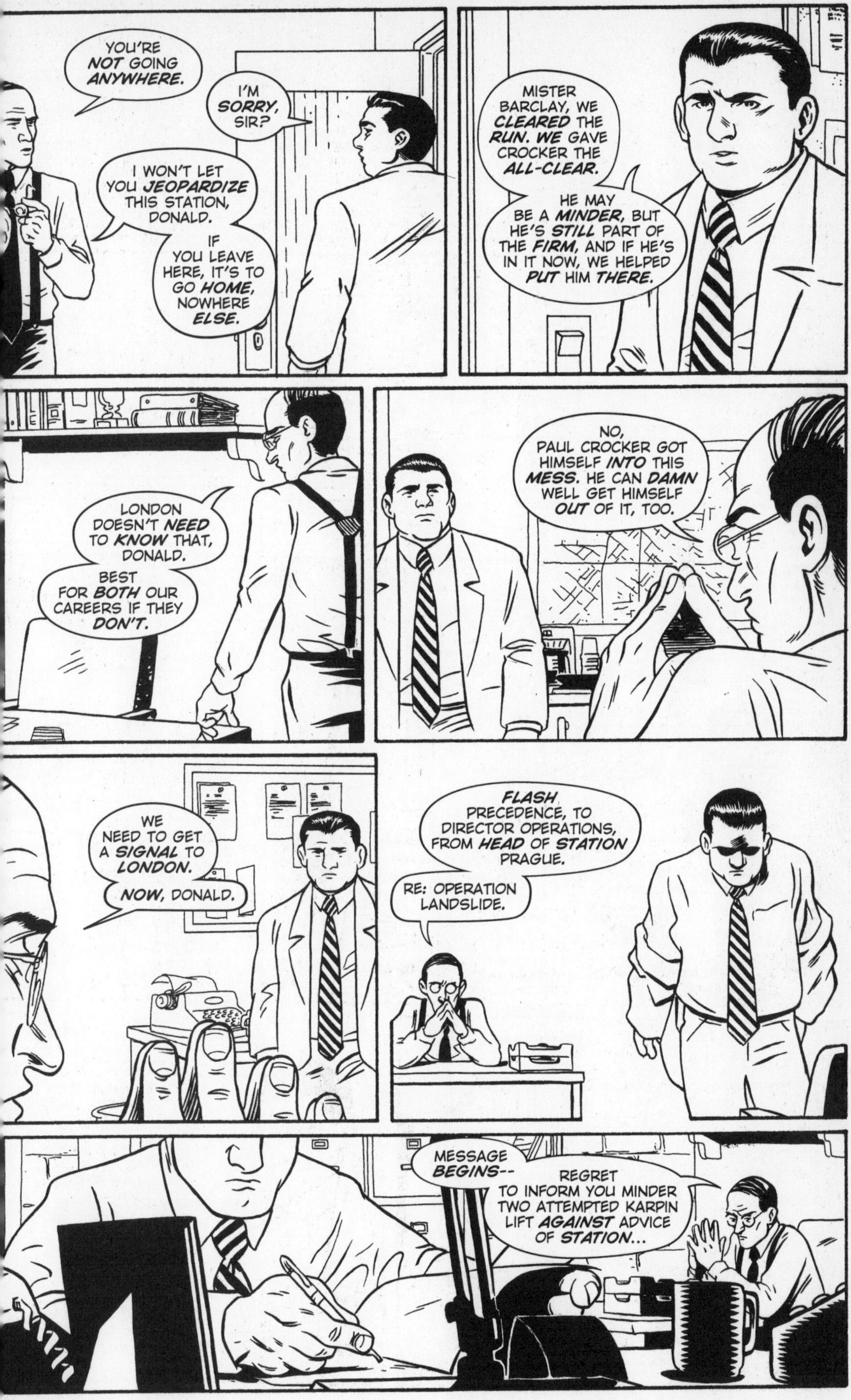

YOU'RE NOT GOING ANYWHERE.
I'M SORRY, SIR?
I WON'T LET YOU JEOPARDIZE THIS STATION, DONALD.
IF YOU LEAVE HERE, IT'S TO GO HOME, NOWHERE ELSE.
MISTER BARCLAY, WE CLEARED THE RUN. WE GAVE CROCKER THE ALL-CLEAR.
HE MAY BE A MINDER, BUT HE'S STILL PART OF THE FIRM, AND IF HE'S IN IT NOW, WE HELPED PUT HIM THERE.
LONDON DOESN'T NEED TO KNOW THAT, DONALD.
BEST FOR BOTH OUR CAREERS IF THEY DON'T.
NO, PAUL CROCKER GOT HIMSELF INTO THIS MESS. HE CAN DAMN WELL GET HIMSELF OUT OF IT, TOO.
WE NEED TO GET A SIGNAL TO LONDON.
NOW, DONALD.
FLASH PRECEDENCE, TO DIRECTOR OPERATIONS, FROM HEAD OF STATION PRAGUE.
RE: OPERATION LANDSLIDE.
MESSAGE BEGINS--
REGRET TO INFORM YOU MINDER TWO ATTEMPTED KARPIN LIFT AGAINST ADVICE OF STATION...

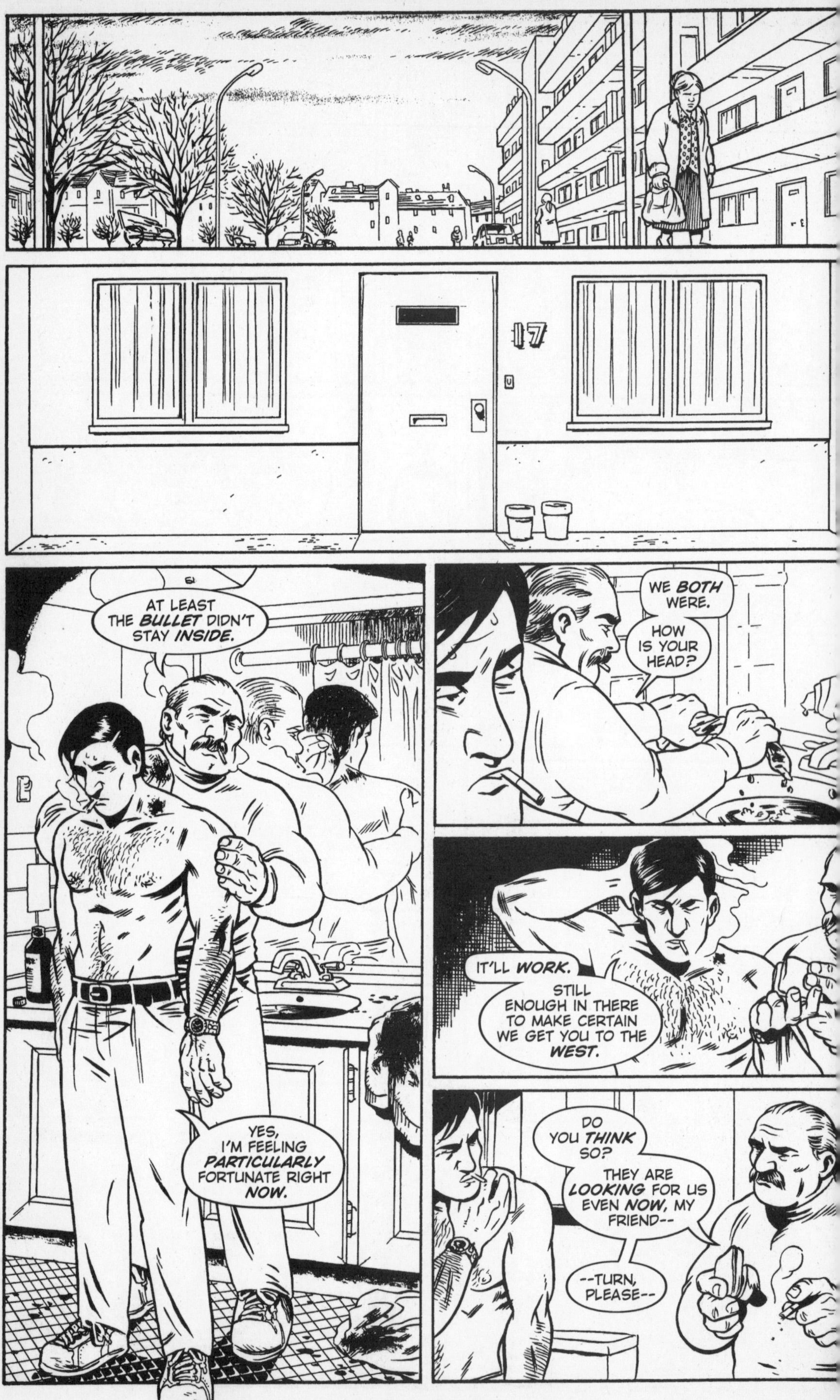
17
AT LEAST THE BULLET DIDN'T STAY INSIDE.
YES, I'M FEELING PARTICULARLY FORTUNATE RIGHT NOW.
WE BOTH WERE.
HOW IS YOUR HEAD?
IT'LL WORK.
STILL ENOUGH IN THERE TO MAKE CERTAIN WE GET YOU TO THE WEST.
DO YOU THINK SO?
THEY ARE LOOKING FOR US EVEN NOW, MY FRIEND--
--TURN, PLEASE--

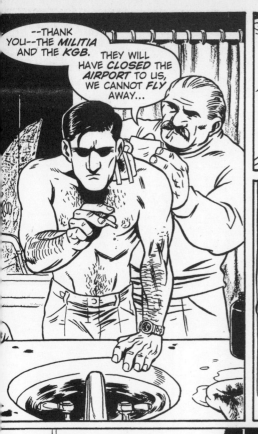

--THANK YOU--THE *MILITIA* AND THE *KGB*. THEY WILL HAVE *CLOSED* THE *AIRPORT* TO US, WE CANNOT *FLY* AWAY...

...THE *TRAINS* WILL BE STOPPED AT THE *BORDER* AS A MATTER OF *COURSE*...

...AND THERE ARE NO *BOATS* TO TAKE US TO THE WEST.

THERE *ARE*, HOWEVER, STILL *BULLETS* IN YOUR *GUN*.

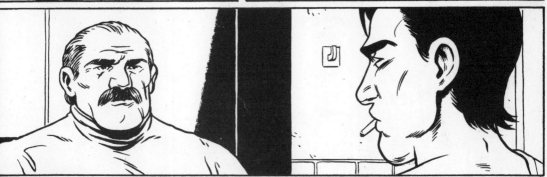

I'M NOT BLOODY DYING IN *PRAGUE*, AND *NEITHER* ARE *YOU*.

THE *STATION* WILL MAKE *CONTACT*...

...WE JUST NEED TO *WAIT*.

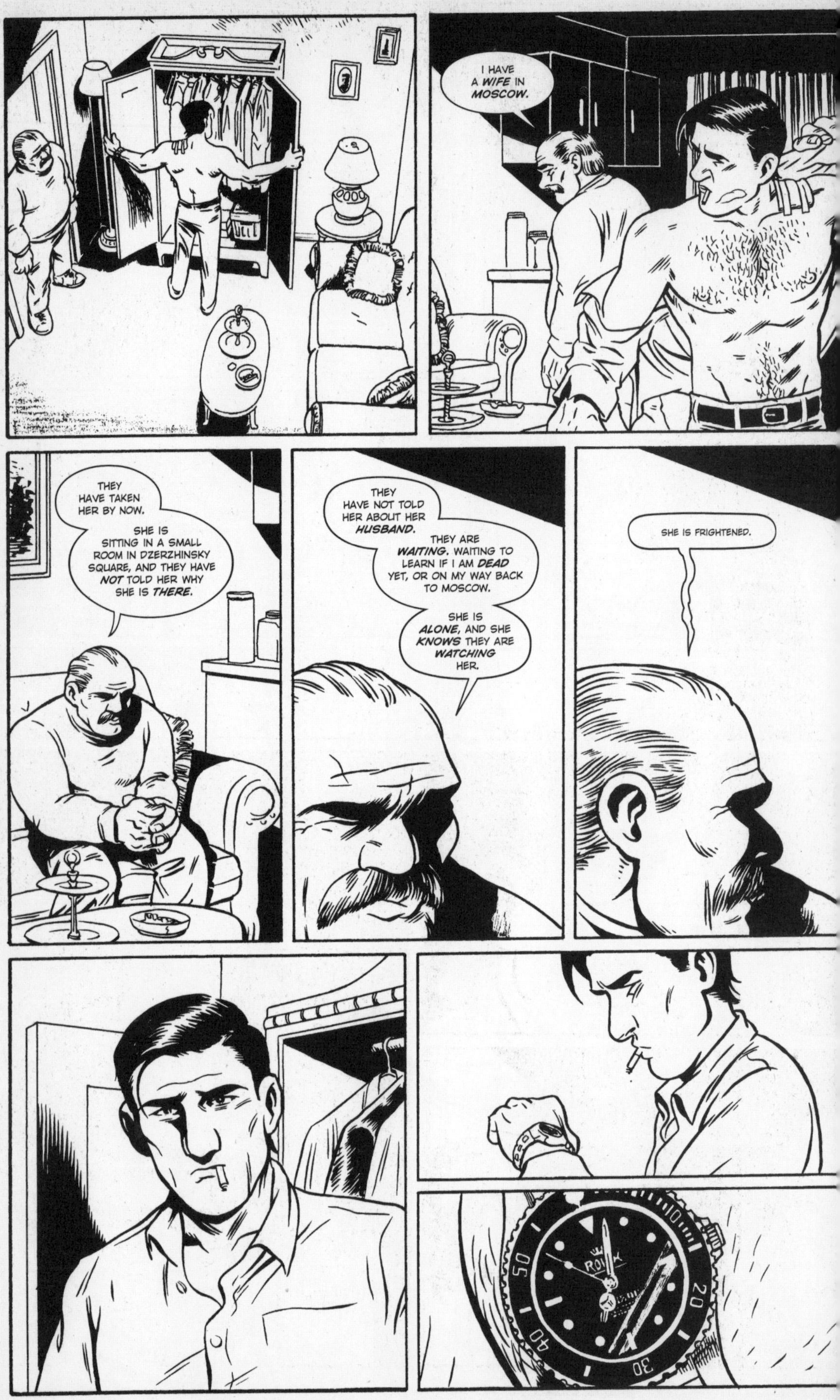

I HAVE A WIFE IN MOSCOW.
THEY HAVE TAKEN HER BY NOW.
SHE IS SITTING IN A SMALL ROOM IN DZERZHINSKY SQUARE, AND THEY HAVE NOT TOLD HER WHY SHE IS THERE.
THEY HAVE NOT TOLD HER ABOUT HER HUSBAND.
THEY ARE WAITING. WAITING TO LEARN IF I AM DEAD YET, OR ON MY WAY BACK TO MOSCOW.
SHE IS ALONE, AND SHE KNOWS THEY ARE WATCHING HER.
SHE IS FRIGHTENED.

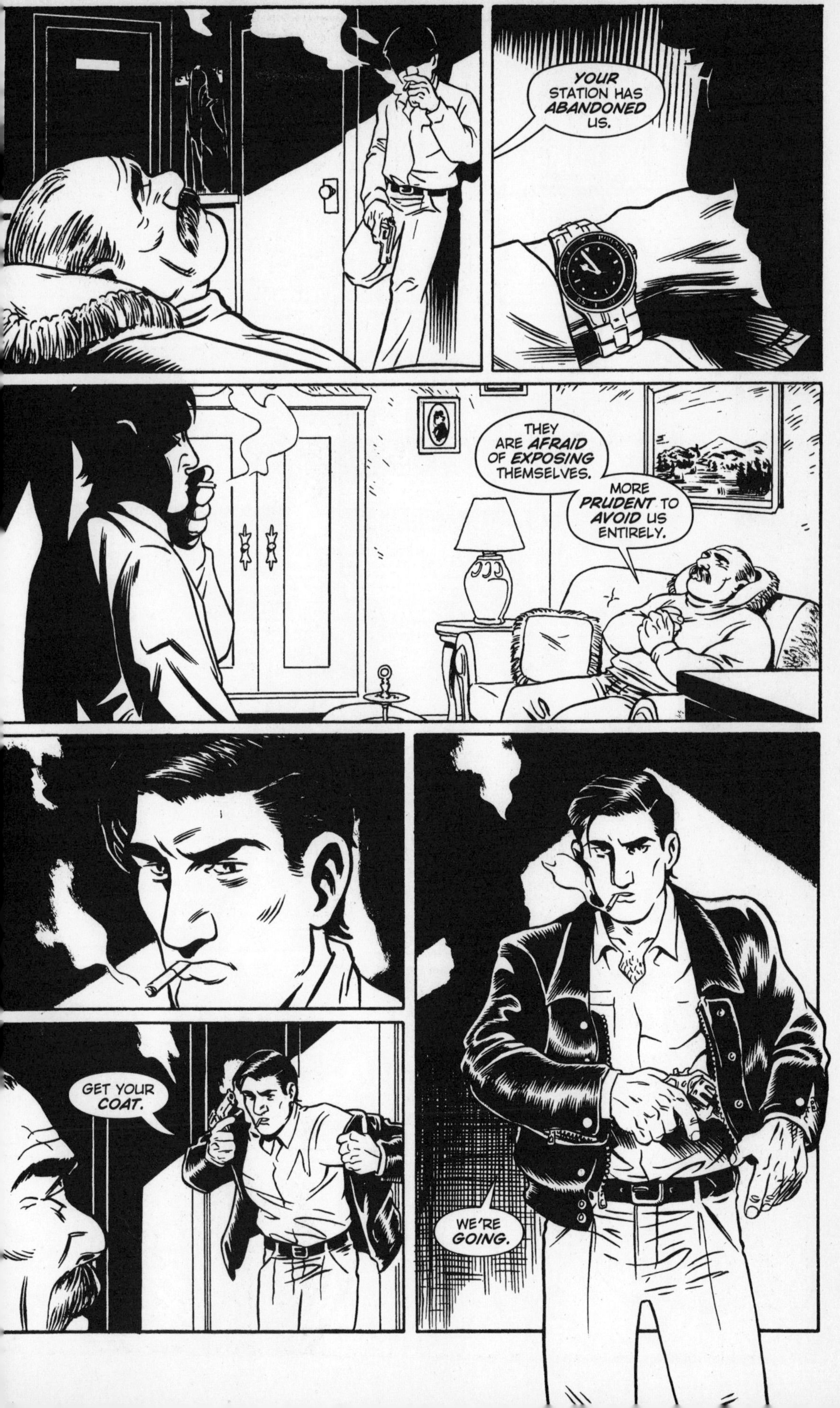
YOUR STATION HAS ABANDONED US.
THEY ARE AFRAID OF EXPOSING THEMSELVES.
MORE PRUDENT TO AVOID US ENTIRELY.
GET YOUR COAT.
WE'RE GOING.

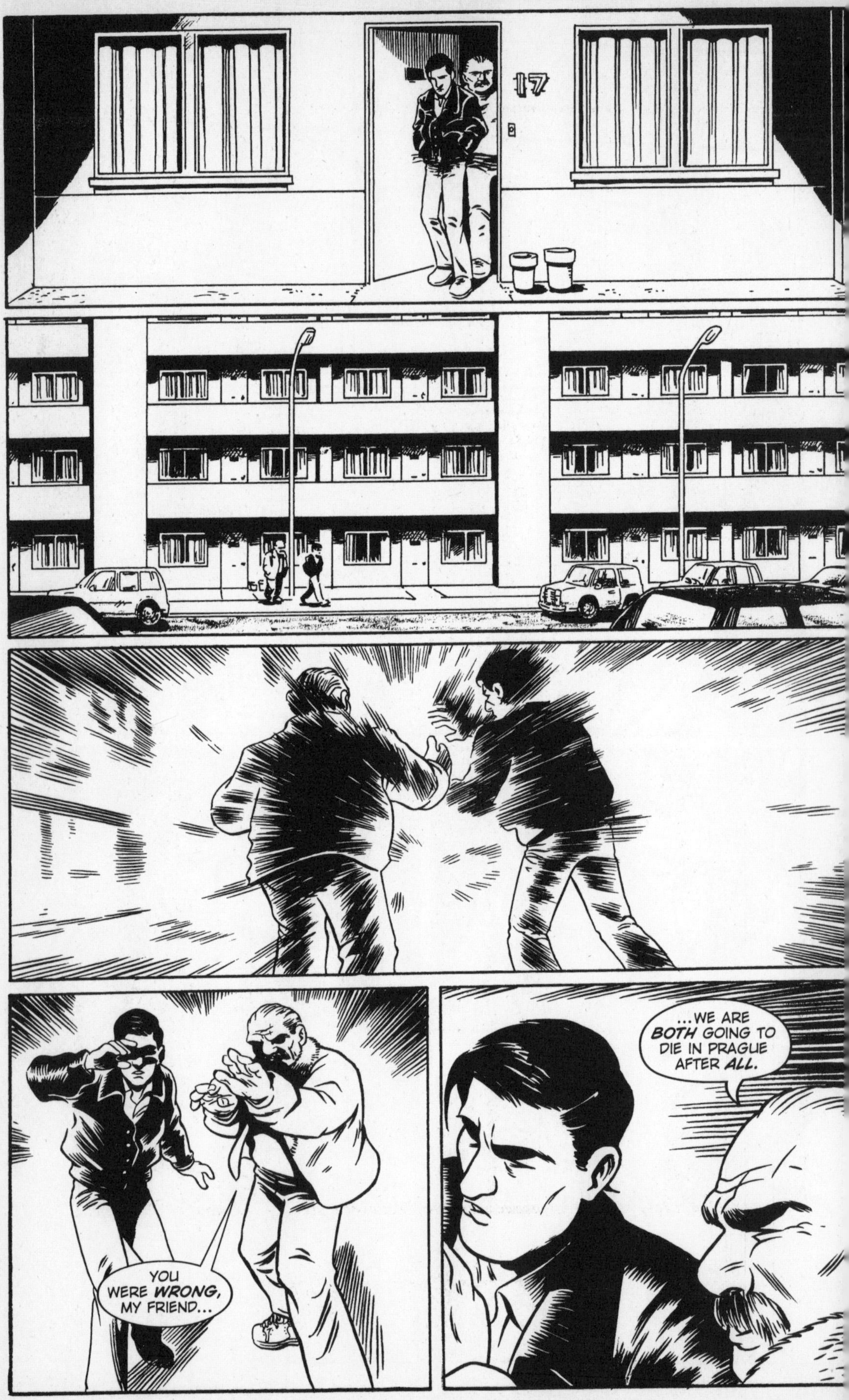
17
YOU WERE WRONG, MY FRIEND...
...WE ARE BOTH GOING TO DIE IN PRAGUE AFTER ALL.

CHAPTER 3

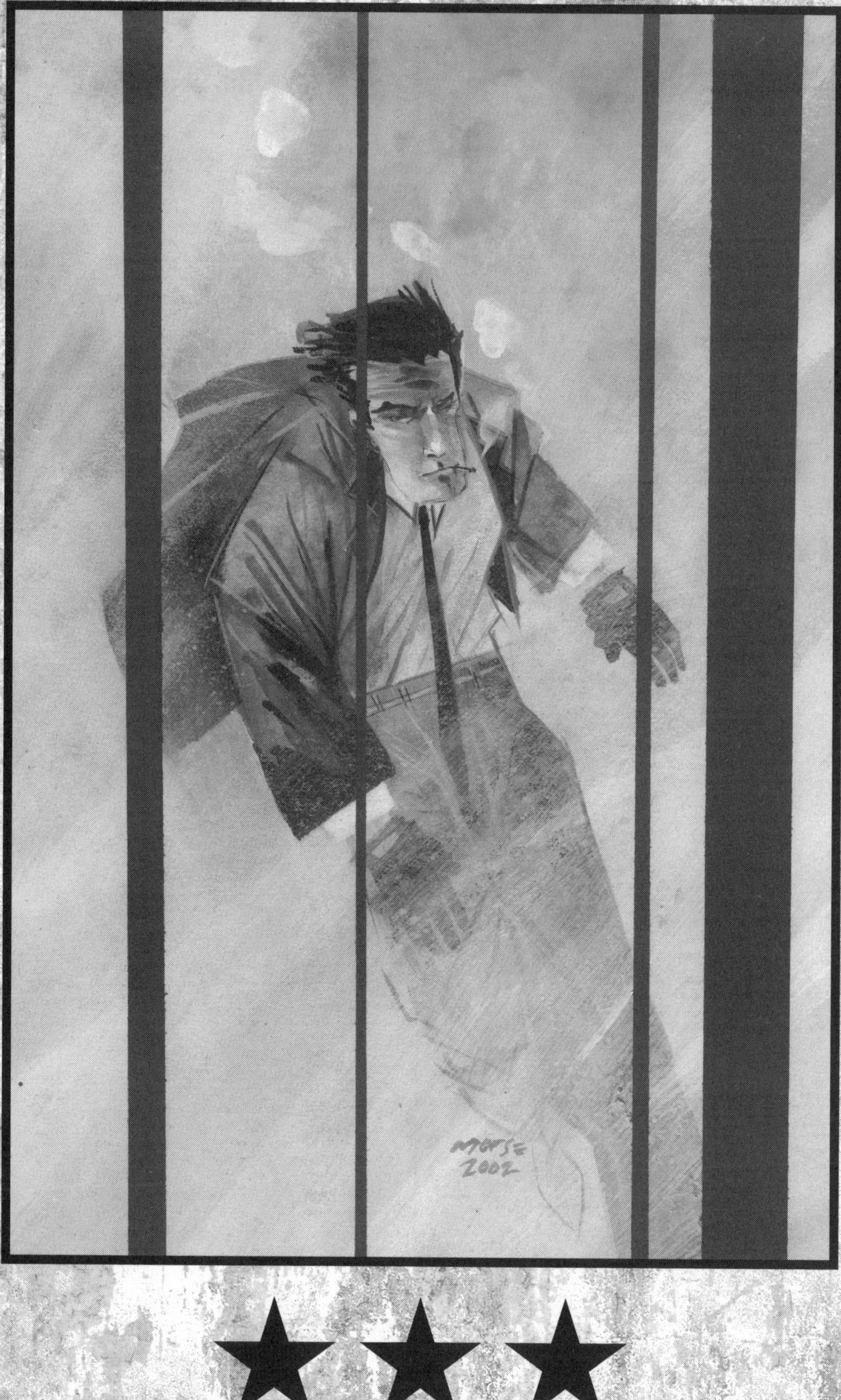

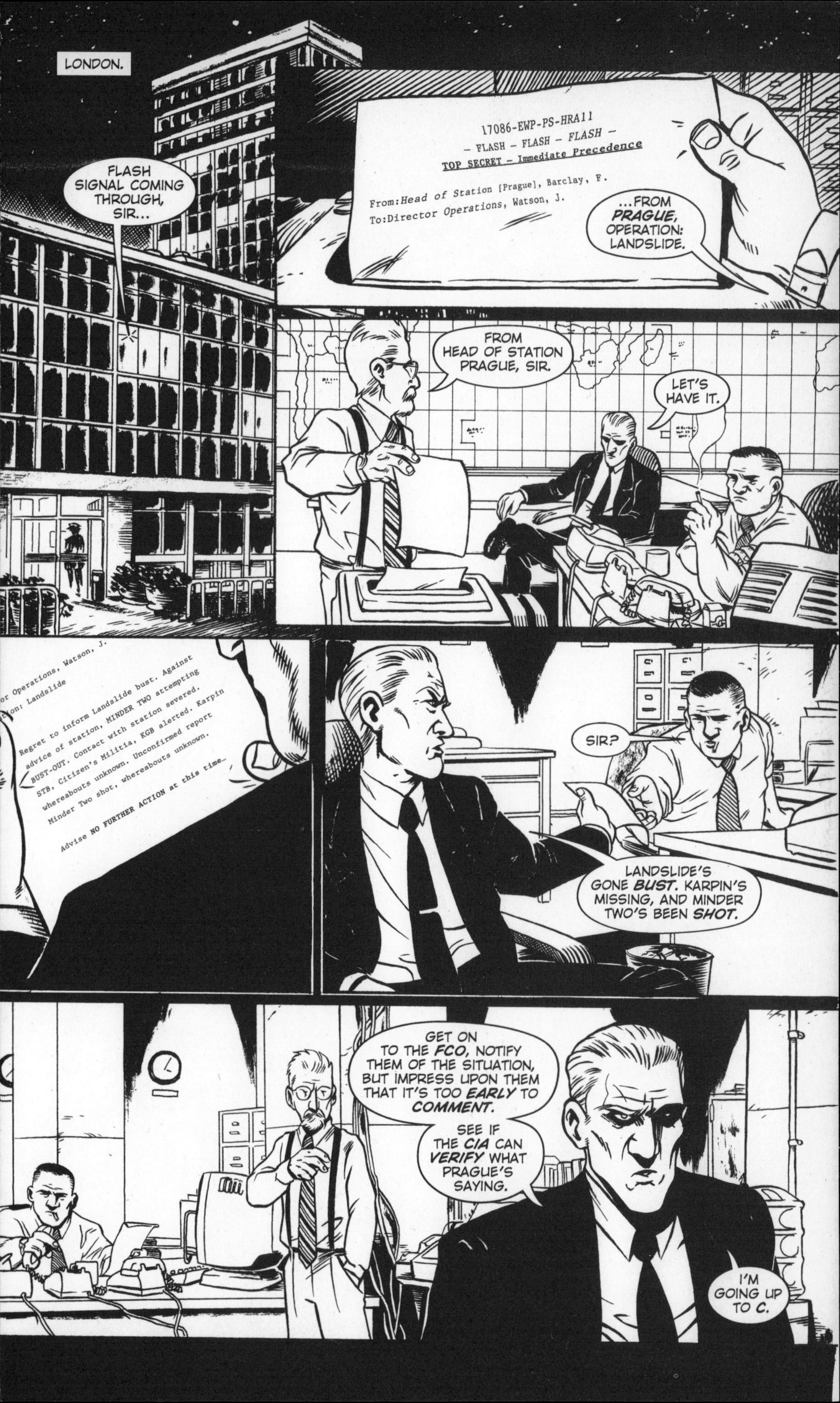
LONDON.
FLASH SIGNAL COMING THROUGH, SIR...
17086-EWP-PS-HRA11
– FLASH – FLASH – FLASH –
TOP SECRET – Immediate Precedence
From:Head of Station [Prague], Barclay, F.
To:Director Operations, Watson, J.
...FROM PRAGUE, OPERATION: LANDSLIDE.
FROM HEAD OF STATION PRAGUE, SIR.
LET'S HAVE IT.
or Operations, Watson, J.
on: Landslide
Regret to inform Landslide bust. Against
advice of station, MINDER TWO attempting
BUST-OUT. Contact with station severed.
STB, Citizen's Militia, KGB alerted. Karpin
whereabouts unknown. Unconfirmed report
Minder Two shot, whereabouts unknown.
Advise NO FURTHER ACTION at this time...
SIR?
LANDSLIDE'S GONE BUST. KARPIN'S MISSING, AND MINDER TWO'S BEEN SHOT.
GET ON TO THE FCO, NOTIFY THEM OF THE SITUATION, BUT IMPRESS UPON THEM THAT IT'S TOO EARLY TO COMMENT.
SEE IF THE CIA CAN VERIFY WHAT PRAGUE'S SAYING.
I'M GOING UP TO C.

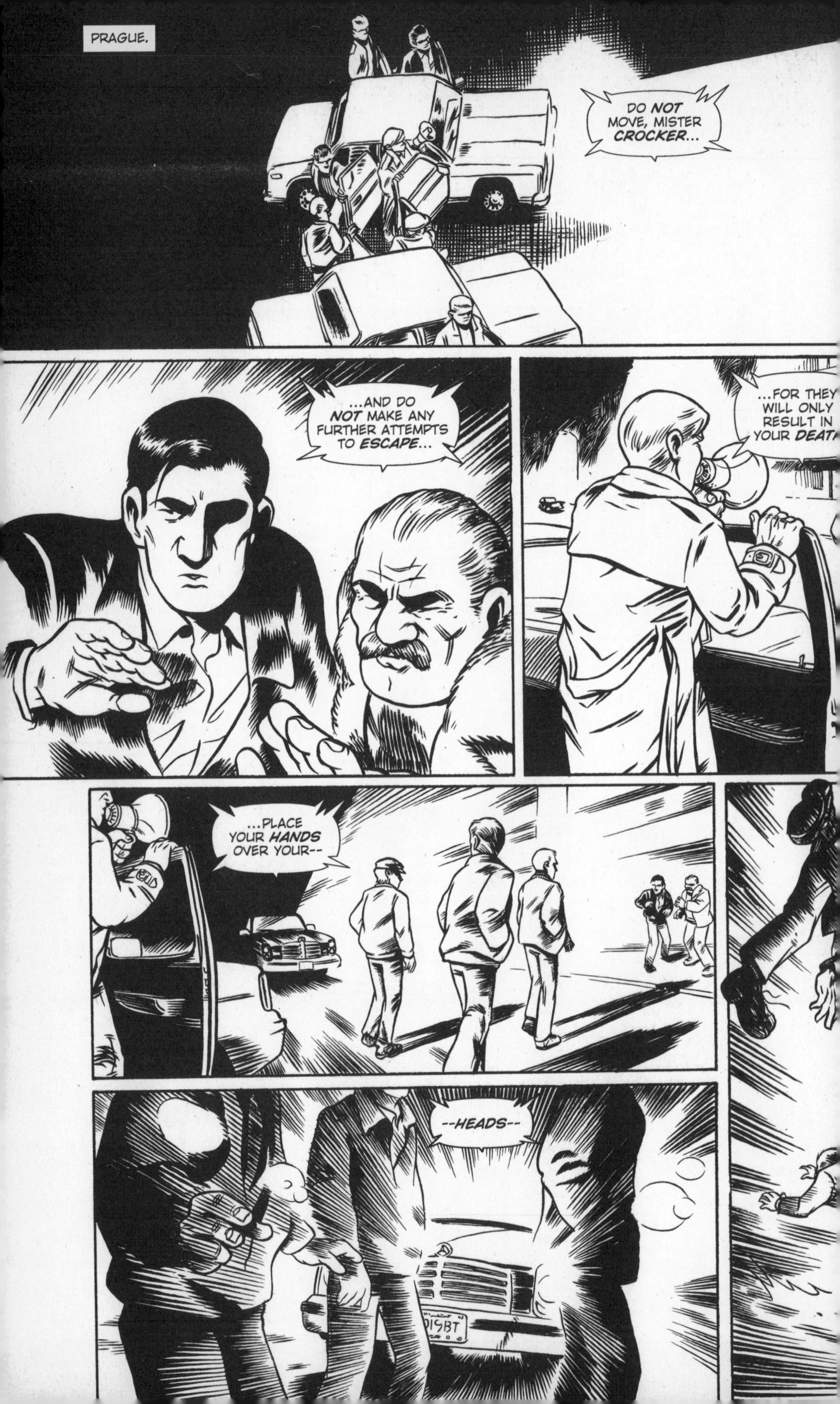
PRAGUE.
DO NOT MOVE, MISTER CROCKER...
...AND DO NOT MAKE ANY FURTHER ATTEMPTS TO ESCAPE...
...FOR THEY WILL ONLY RESULT IN YOUR DEAT
...PLACE YOUR HANDS OVER YOUR--
--HEADS--

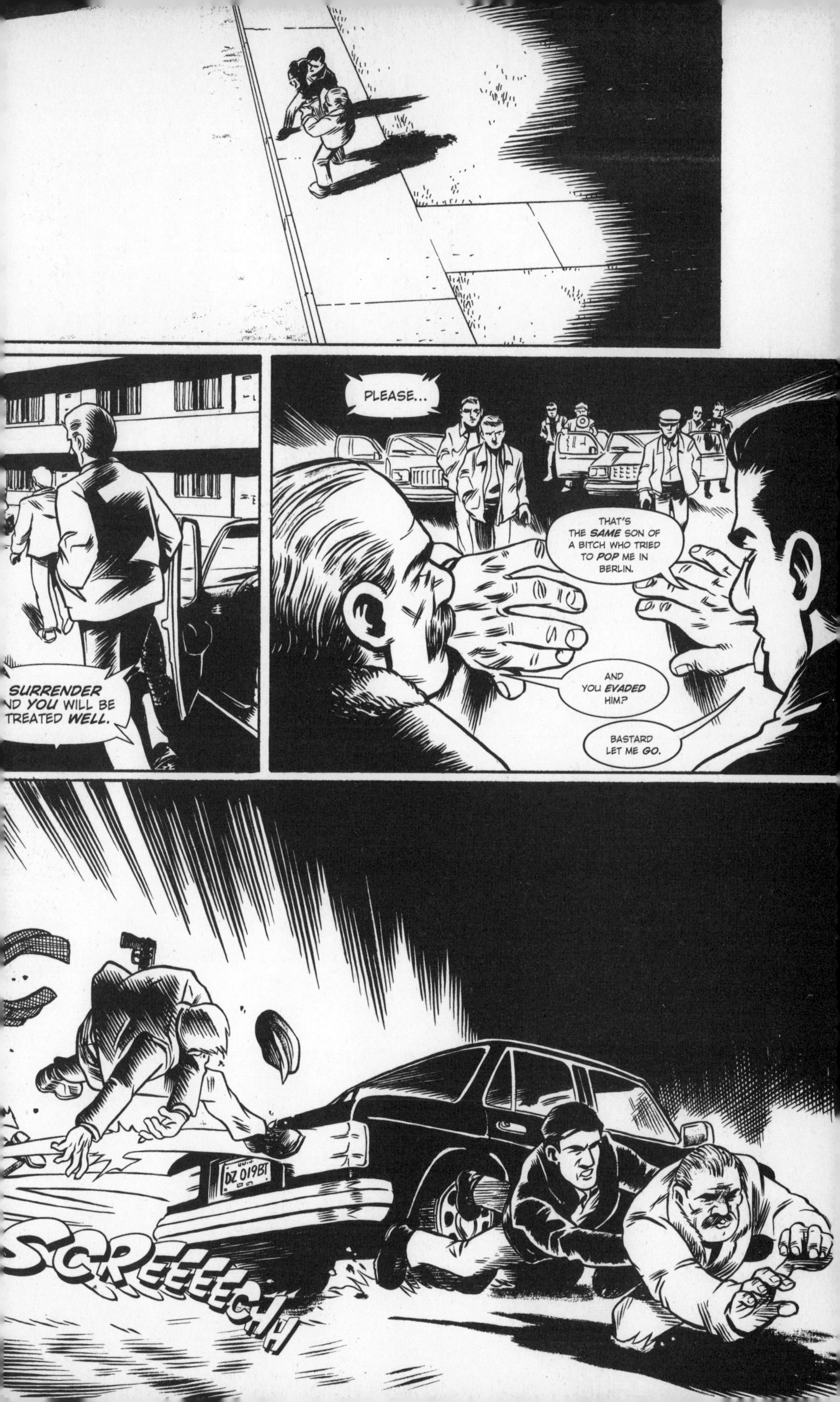
SURRENDER
ND YOU WILL BE
TREATED WELL.
PLEASE...
THAT'S THE SAME SON OF A BITCH WHO TRIED TO POP ME IN BERLIN.
AND YOU EVADED HIM?
BASTARD LET ME GO.
DZ 019BT
SCREEEEECH

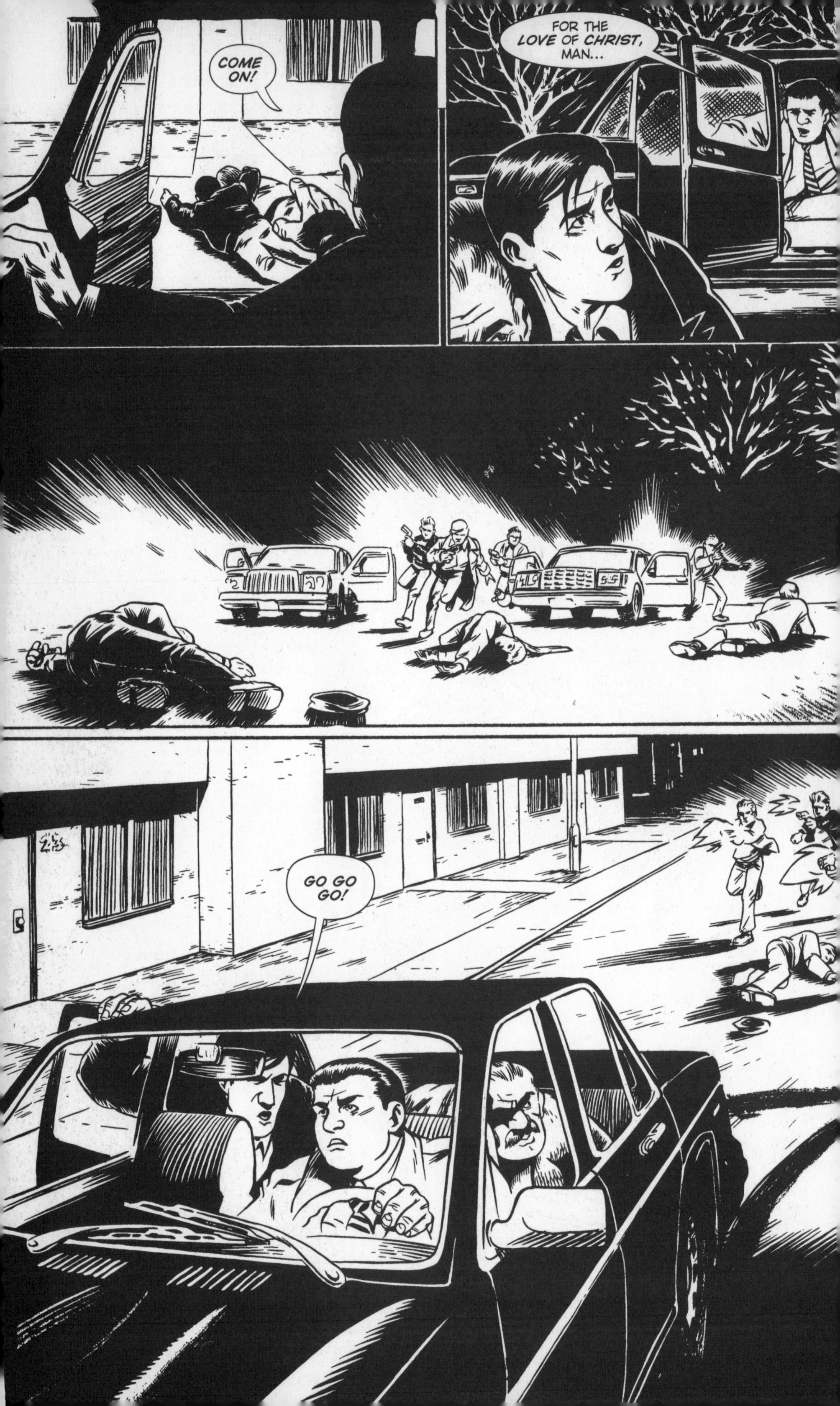
COME ON!
FOR THE LOVE OF CHRIST, MAN...
GO GO GO!

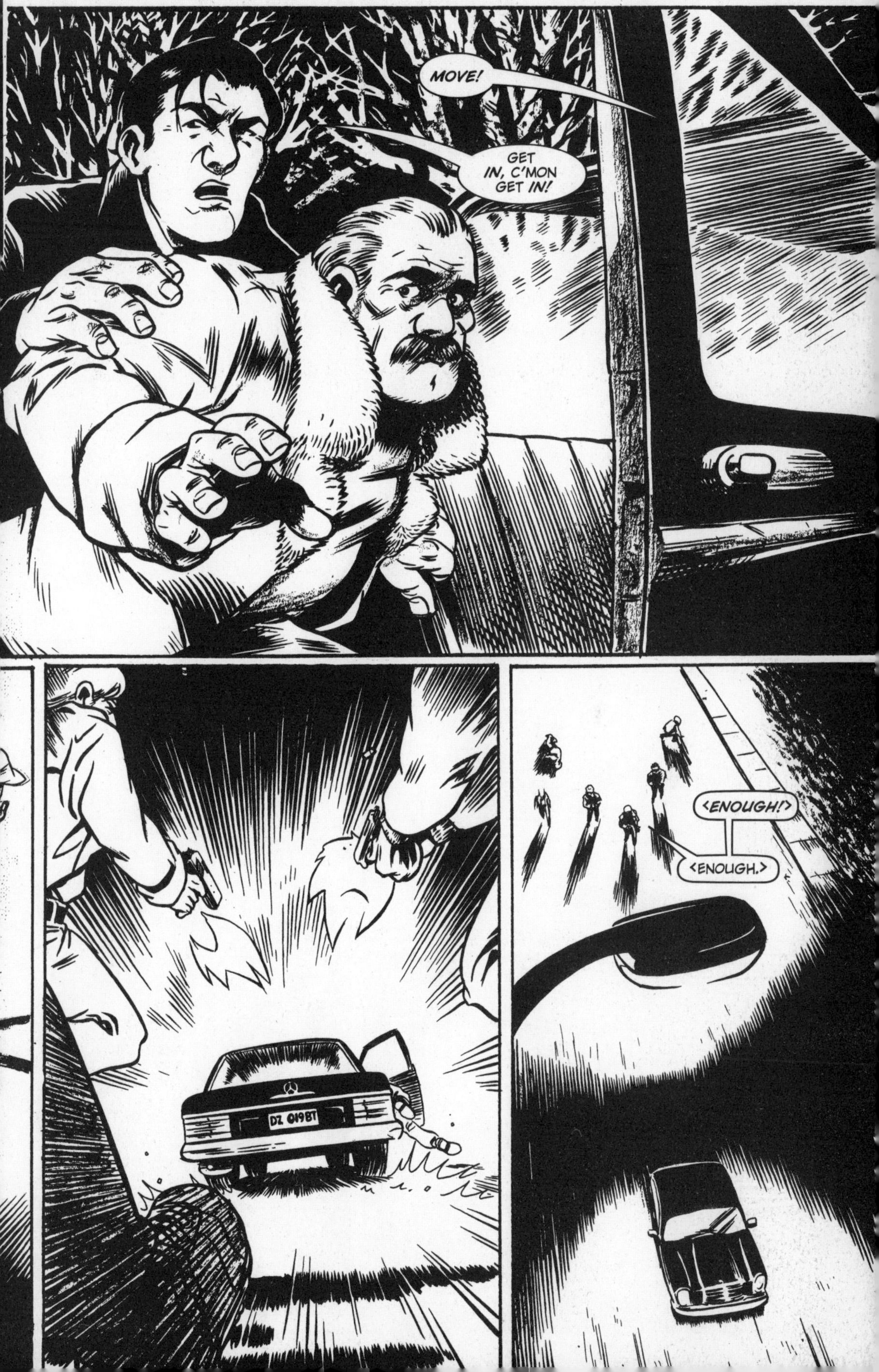
MOVE!
GET IN, C'MON GET IN!
<ENOUGH!>
<ENOUGH.>

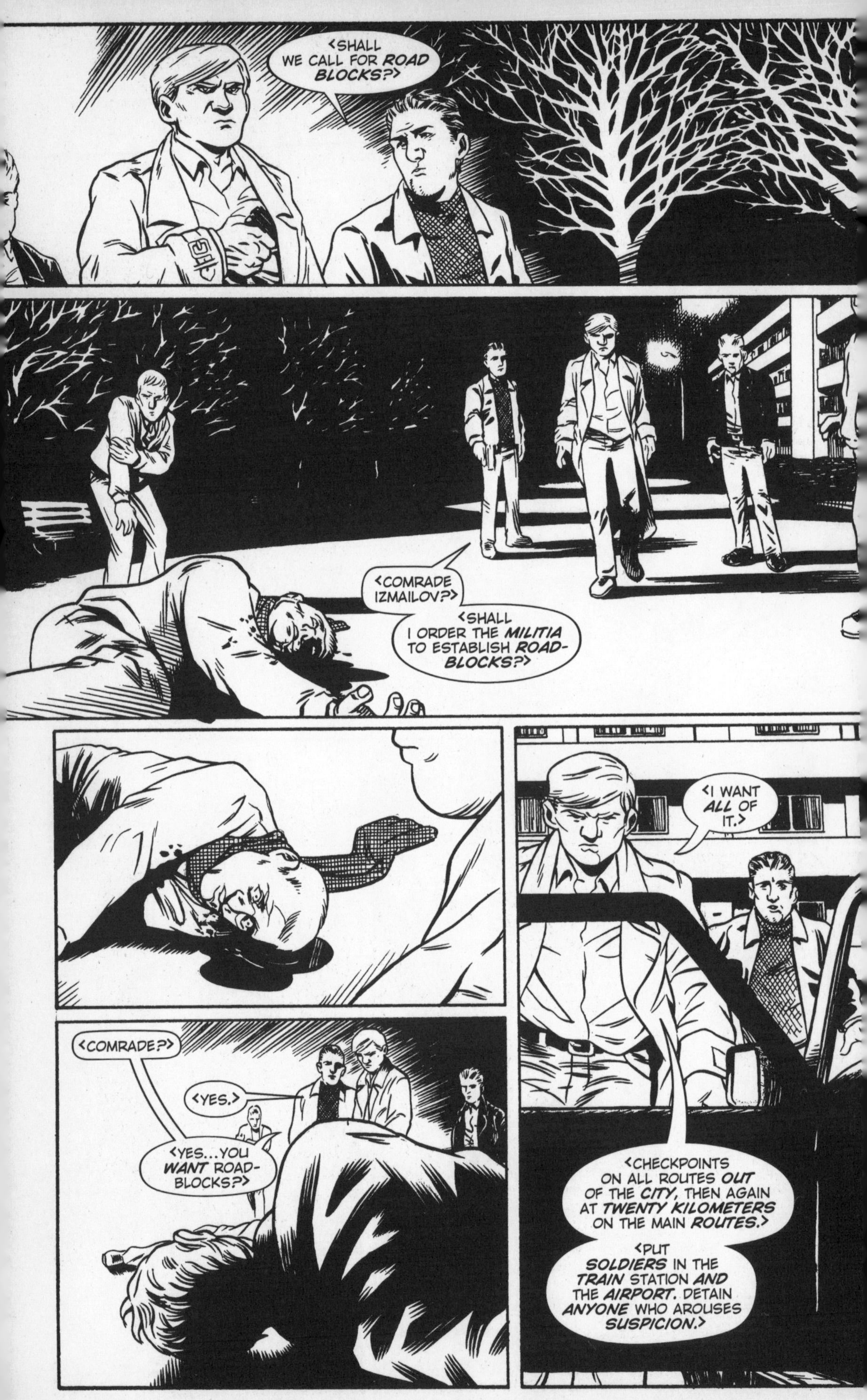
<SHALL WE CALL FOR *ROAD BLOCKS?*>
<COMRADE IZMAILOV?>
<SHALL I ORDER THE *MILITIA* TO ESTABLISH *ROAD-BLOCKS?*>
<COMRADE?>
<YES.>
<YES...YOU *WANT* ROAD-BLOCKS?>
<I WANT *ALL* OF IT.>
<CHECKPOINTS ON ALL ROUTES *OUT* OF THE *CITY*, THEN AGAIN AT *TWENTY KILOMETERS* ON THE MAIN *ROUTES*.>
<PUT *SOLDIERS* IN THE *TRAIN* STATION *AND* THE *AIRPORT*. DETAIN *ANYONE* WHO AROUSES *SUSPICION*.>

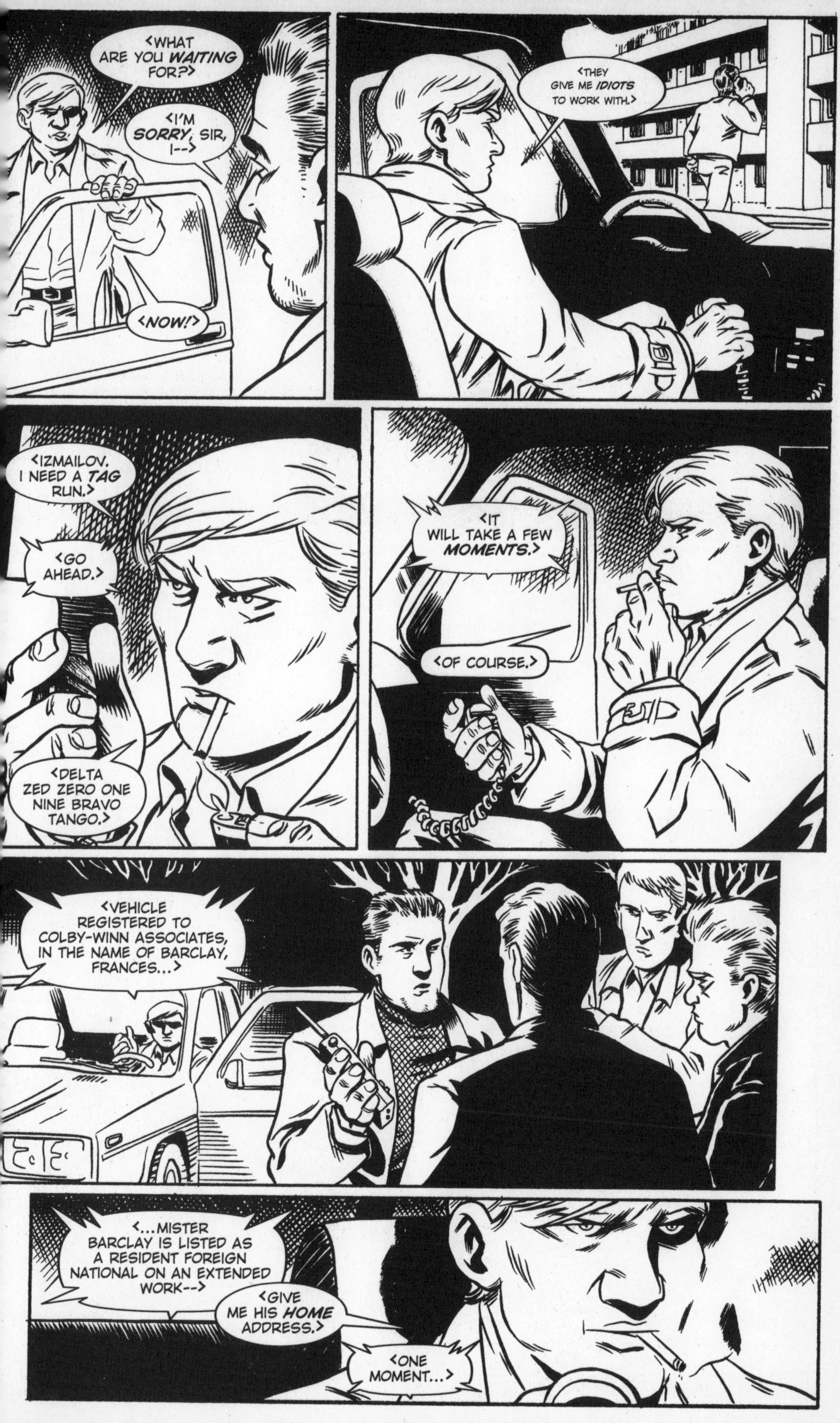

<WHAT ARE YOU *WAITING* FOR?>
<I'M *SORRY*, SIR, I-->
<*NOW!*>
<THEY GIVE ME *IDIOTS* TO WORK WITH.>
<IZMAILOV. I NEED A *TAG* RUN.>
<GO AHEAD.>
<DELTA ZED ZERO ONE NINE BRAVO TANGO.>
<IT WILL TAKE A FEW *MOMENTS*.>
<OF COURSE.>
<VEHICLE REGISTERED TO COLBY-WINN ASSOCIATES, IN THE NAME OF BARCLAY, FRANCES...>
<...MISTER BARCLAY IS LISTED AS A RESIDENT FOREIGN NATIONAL ON AN EXTENDED WORK-->
<GIVE ME HIS *HOME* ADDRESS.>
<ONE MOMENT...>

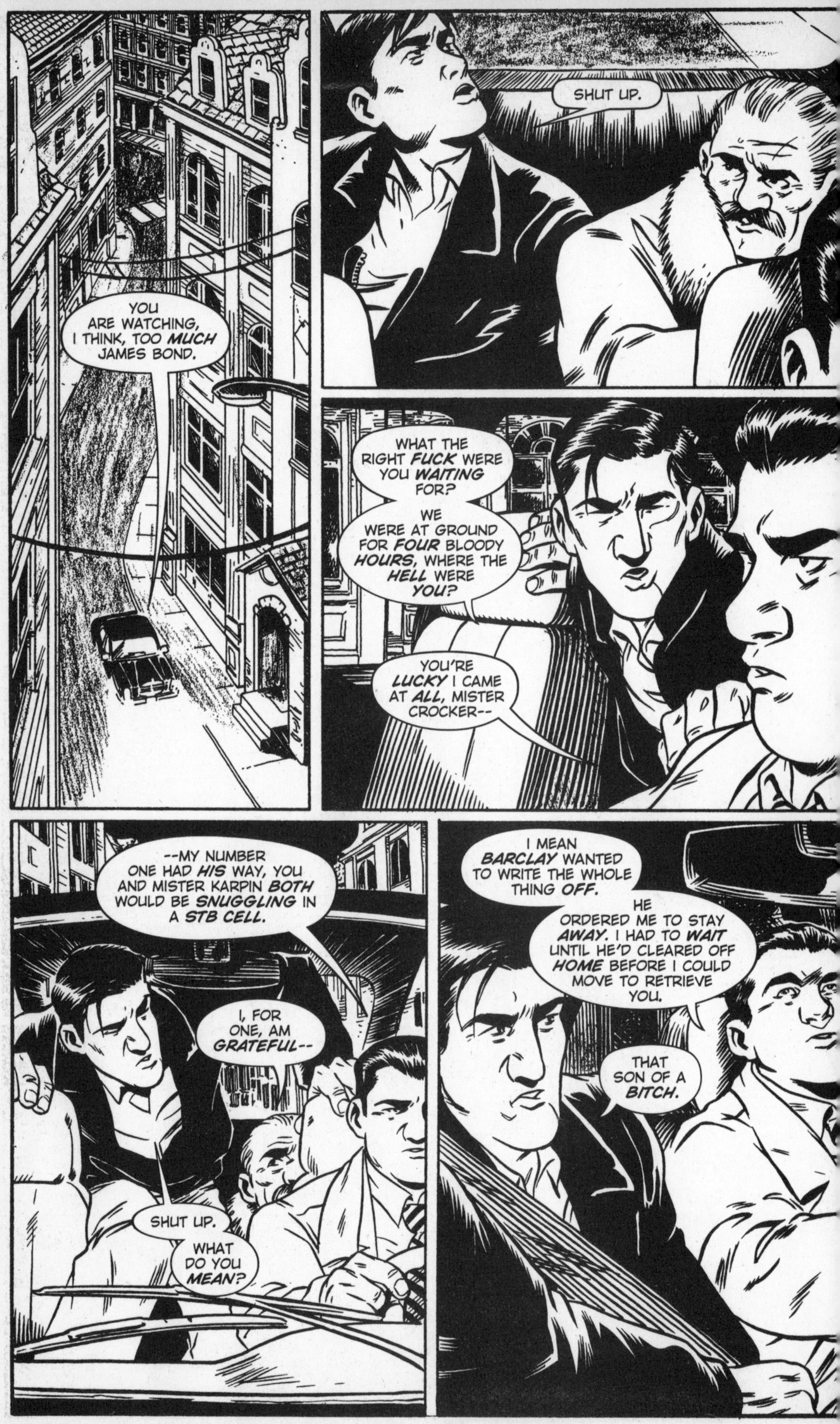
YOU ARE WATCHING, I THINK, TOO MUCH JAMES BOND.
SHUT UP.
WHAT THE RIGHT FUCK WERE YOU WAITING FOR?
WE WERE AT GROUND FOR FOUR BLOODY HOURS, WHERE THE HELL WERE YOU?
YOU'RE LUCKY I CAME AT ALL, MISTER CROCKER--
--MY NUMBER ONE HAD HIS WAY, YOU AND MISTER KARPIN BOTH WOULD BE SNUGGLING IN A STB CELL.
I, FOR ONE, AM GRATEFUL--
SHUT UP.
WHAT DO YOU MEAN?
I MEAN BARCLAY WANTED TO WRITE THE WHOLE THING OFF.
HE ORDERED ME TO STAY AWAY. I HAD TO WAIT UNTIL HE'D CLEARED OFF HOME BEFORE I COULD MOVE TO RETRIEVE YOU.
THAT SON OF A BITCH.

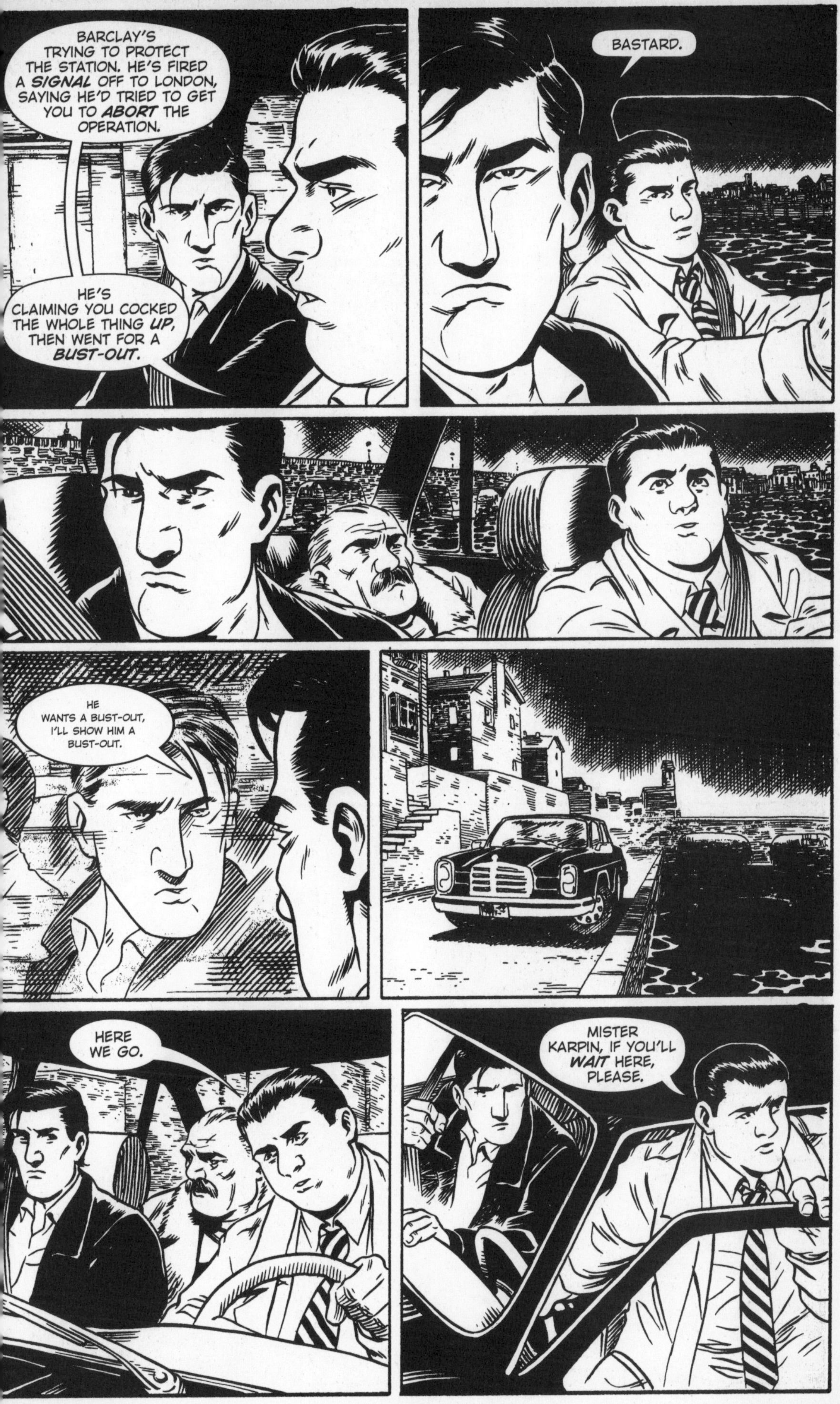
BARCLAY'S TRYING TO PROTECT THE STATION. HE'S FIRED A SIGNAL OFF TO LONDON, SAYING HE'D TRIED TO GET YOU TO ABORT THE OPERATION.
HE'S CLAIMING YOU COCKED THE WHOLE THING UP, THEN WENT FOR A BUST-OUT.
BASTARD.
HE WANTS A BUST-OUT, I'LL SHOW HIM A BUST-OUT.
HERE WE GO.
MISTER KARPIN, IF YOU'LL WAIT HERE, PLEASE.

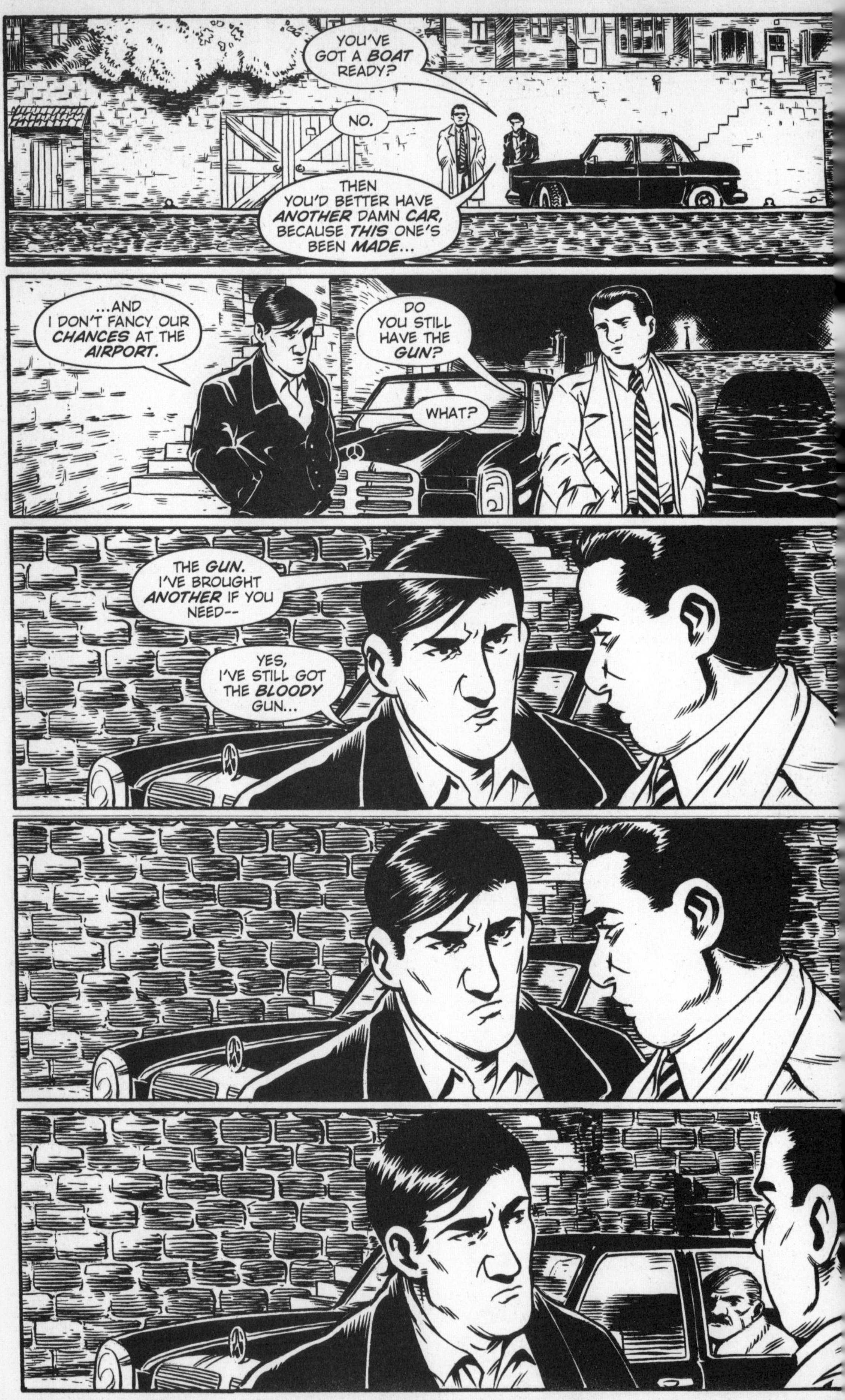
YOU'VE GOT A BOAT READY?
NO.
THEN YOU'D BETTER HAVE ANOTHER DAMN CAR, BECAUSE THIS ONE'S BEEN MADE...
...AND I DON'T FANCY OUR CHANCES AT THE AIRPORT.
DO YOU STILL HAVE THE GUN?
WHAT?
THE GUN. I'VE BROUGHT ANOTHER IF YOU NEED--
YES, I'VE STILL GOT THE BLOODY GUN...

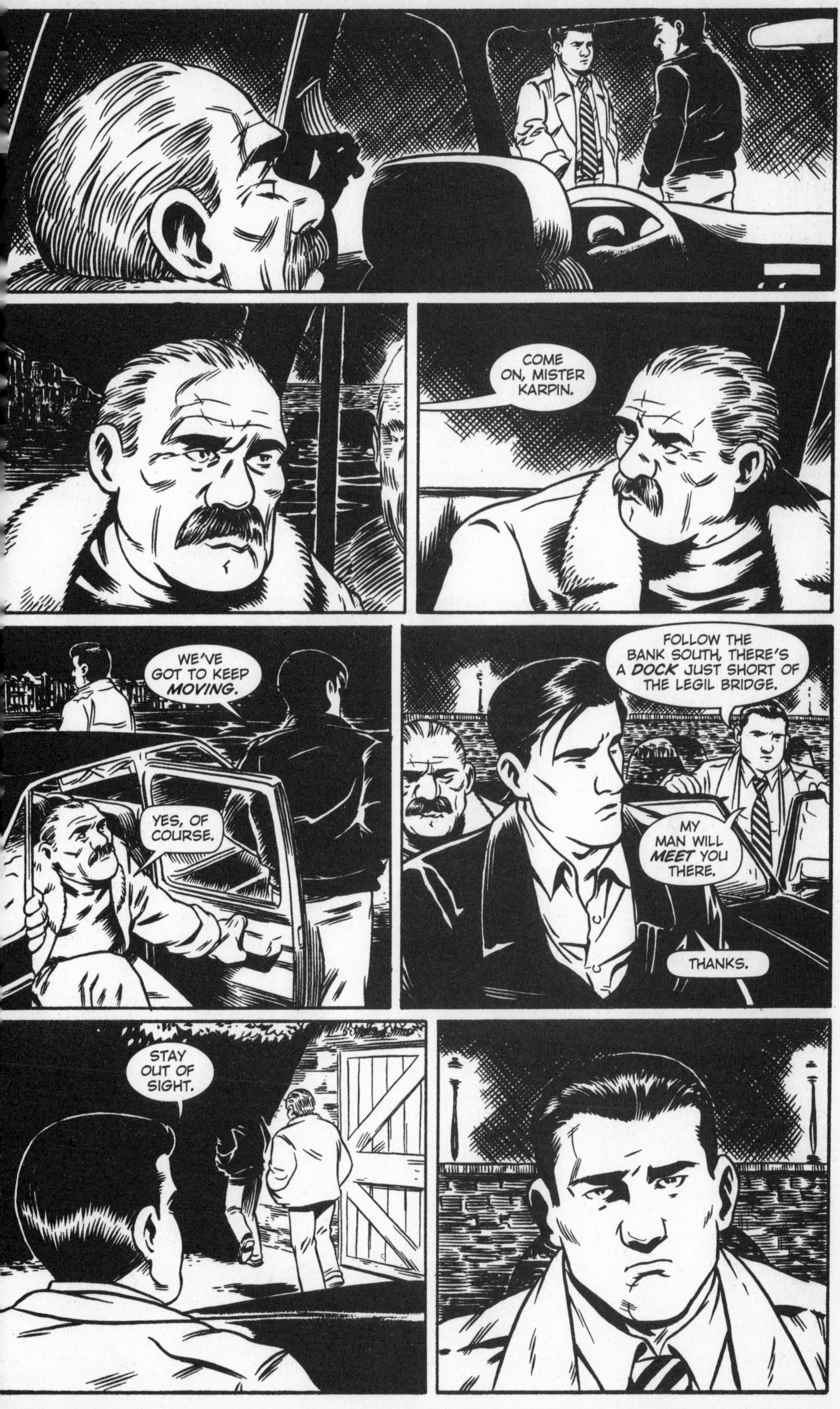
COME ON, MISTER KARPIN.
WE'VE GOT TO KEEP MOVING.
YES, OF COURSE.
FOLLOW THE BANK SOUTH, THERE'S A DOCK JUST SHORT OF THE LEGIL BRIDGE.
MY MAN WILL MEET YOU THERE.
THANKS.
STAY OUT OF SIGHT.

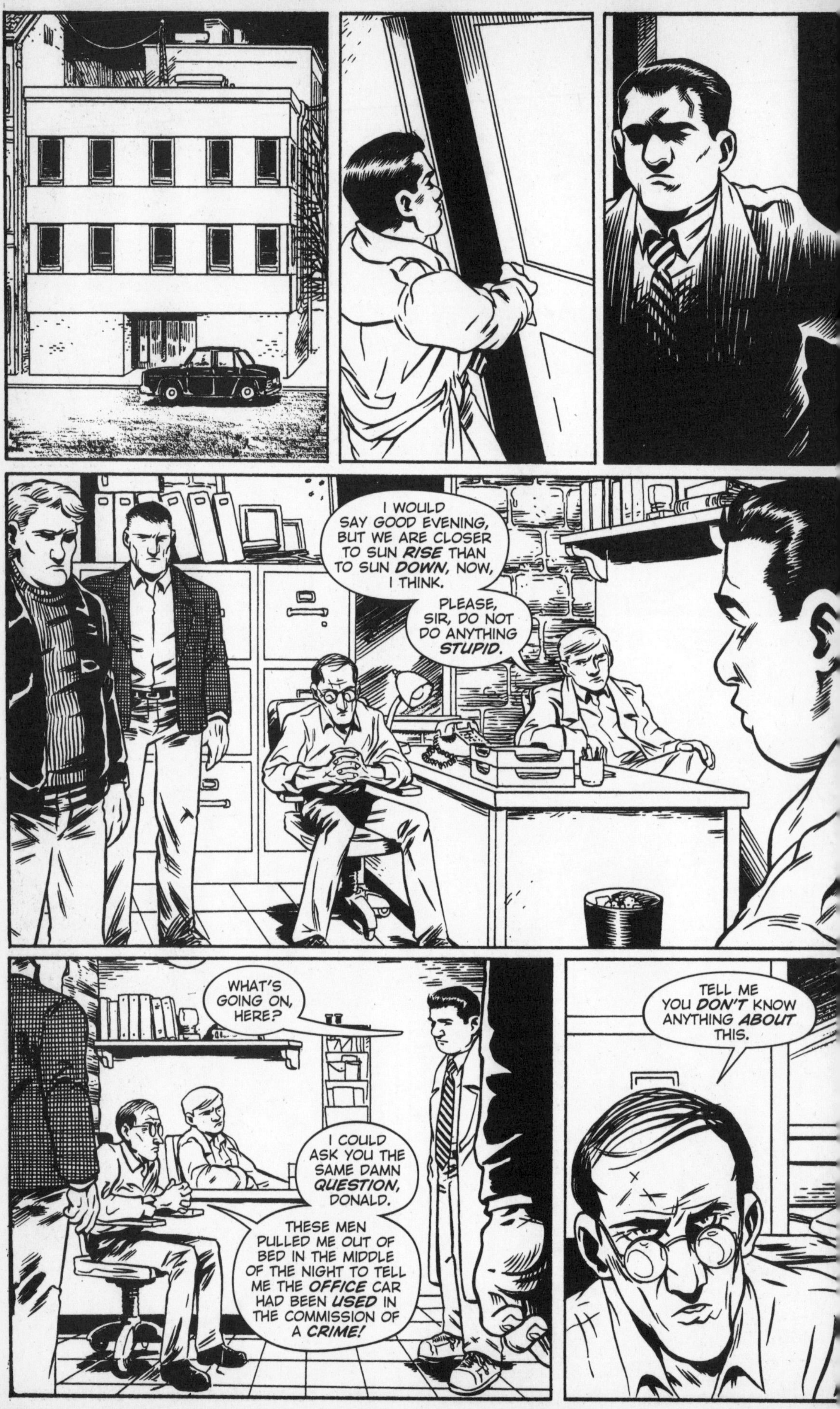
I WOULD SAY GOOD EVENING, BUT WE ARE CLOSER TO SUN *RISE* THAN TO SUN *DOWN,* NOW, I THINK.
PLEASE, SIR, DO NOT DO ANYTHING *STUPID.*
WHAT'S GOING ON, HERE?
I COULD ASK YOU THE SAME DAMN *QUESTION,* DONALD.
THESE MEN PULLED ME OUT OF BED IN THE MIDDLE OF THE NIGHT TO TELL ME THE *OFFICE* CAR HAD BEEN *USED* IN THE COMMISSION OF A *CRIME!*
TELL ME YOU *DON'T* KNOW ANYTHING *ABOUT* THIS.

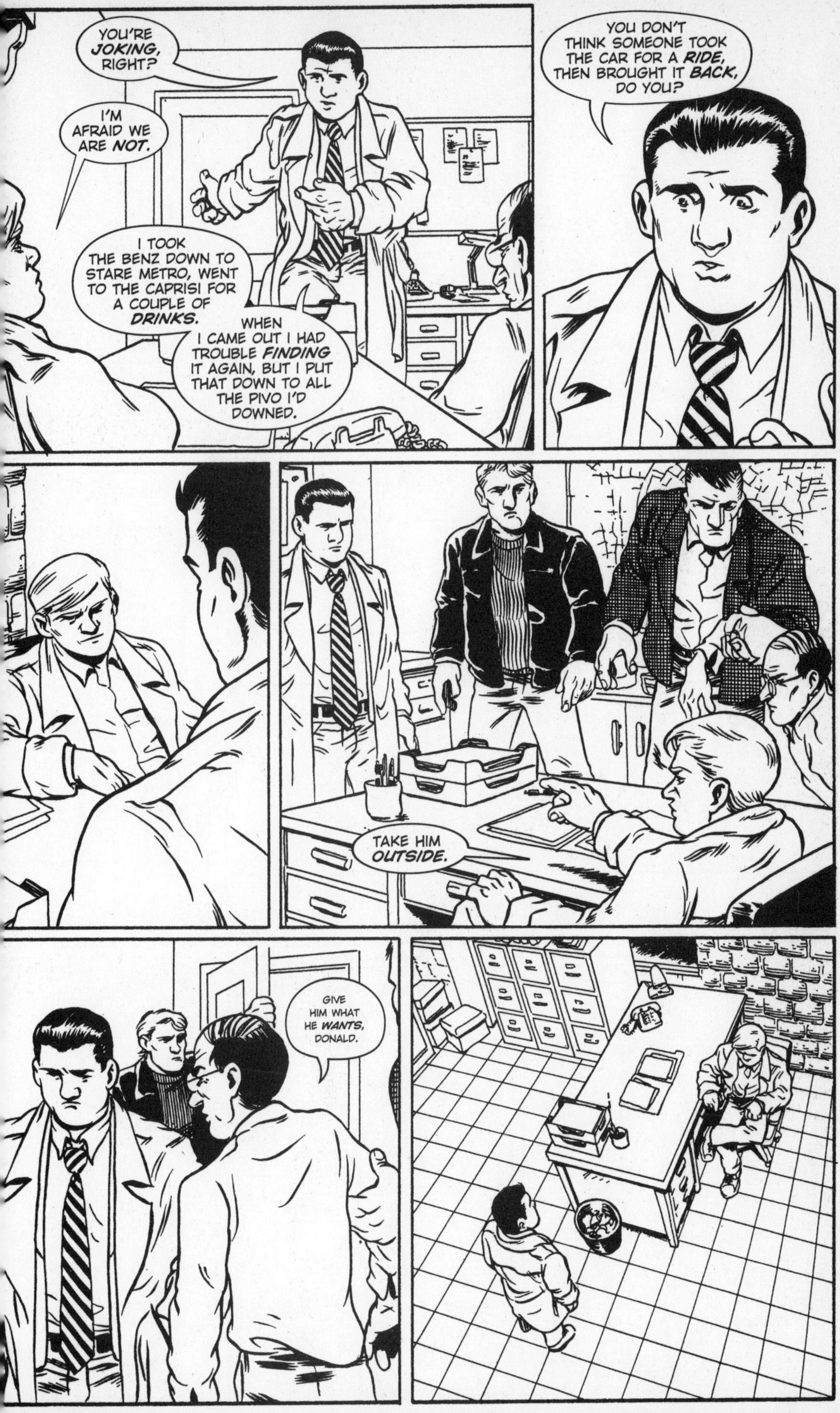
YOU'RE JOKING, RIGHT?
I'M AFRAID WE ARE NOT.
I TOOK THE BENZ DOWN TO STARE METRO, WENT TO THE CAPRISI FOR A COUPLE OF DRINKS.
WHEN I CAME OUT I HAD TROUBLE FINDING IT AGAIN, BUT I PUT THAT DOWN TO ALL THE PIVO I'D DOWNED.
YOU DON'T THINK SOMEONE TOOK THE CAR FOR A RIDE, THEN BROUGHT IT BACK, DO YOU?
TAKE HIM OUTSIDE.
GIVE HIM WHAT HE WANTS, DONALD.

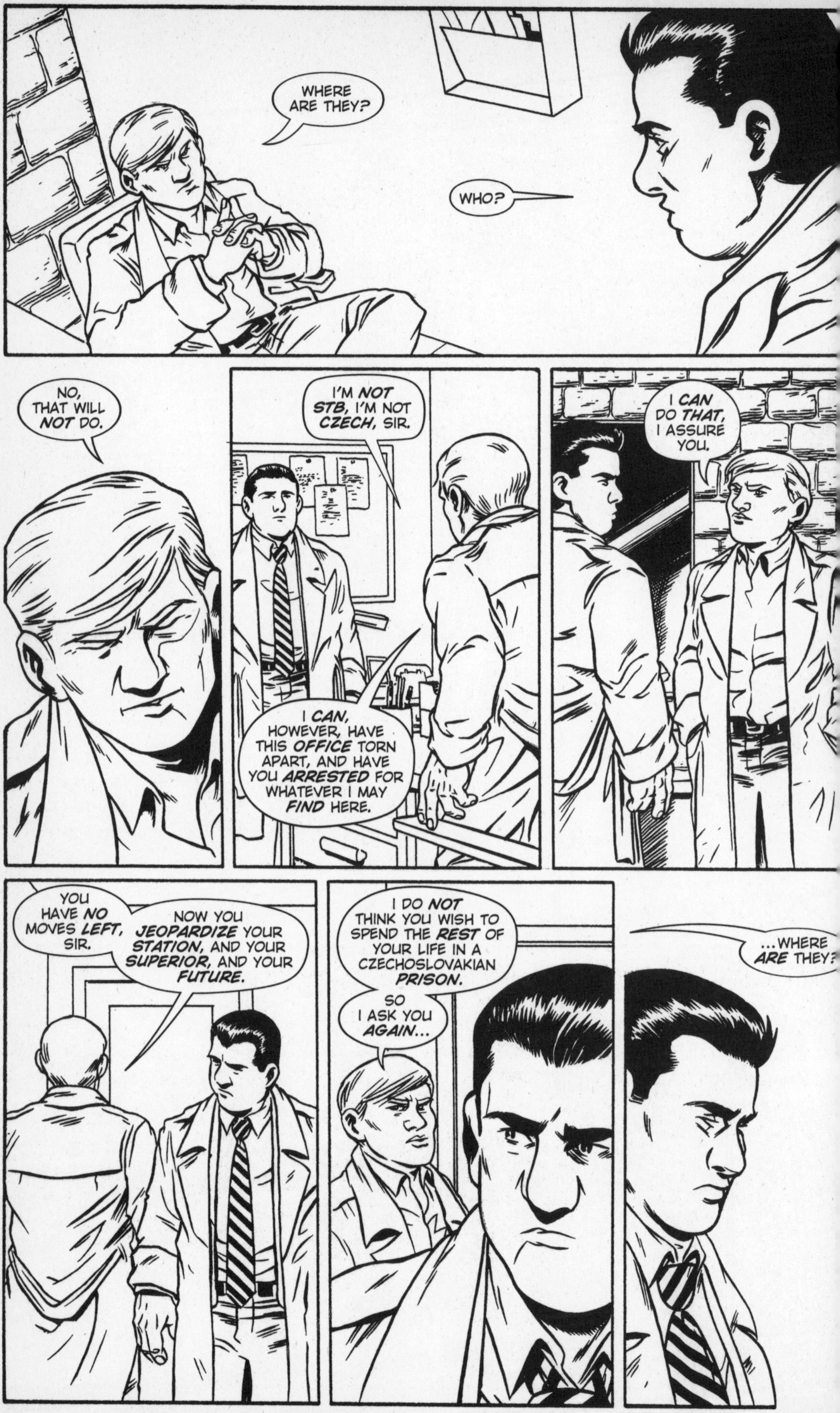
WHERE ARE THEY?
WHO?
NO, THAT WILL NOT DO.
I'M NOT STB, I'M NOT CZECH, SIR.
I CAN, HOWEVER, HAVE THIS OFFICE TORN APART, AND HAVE YOU ARRESTED FOR WHATEVER I MAY FIND HERE.
I CAN DO THAT, I ASSURE YOU.
YOU HAVE NO MOVES LEFT, SIR.
NOW YOU JEOPARDIZE YOUR STATION, AND YOUR SUPERIOR, AND YOUR FUTURE.
I DO NOT THINK YOU WISH TO SPEND THE REST OF YOUR LIFE IN A CZECHOSLOVAKIAN PRISON.
SO I ASK YOU AGAIN...
...WHERE ARE THEY?

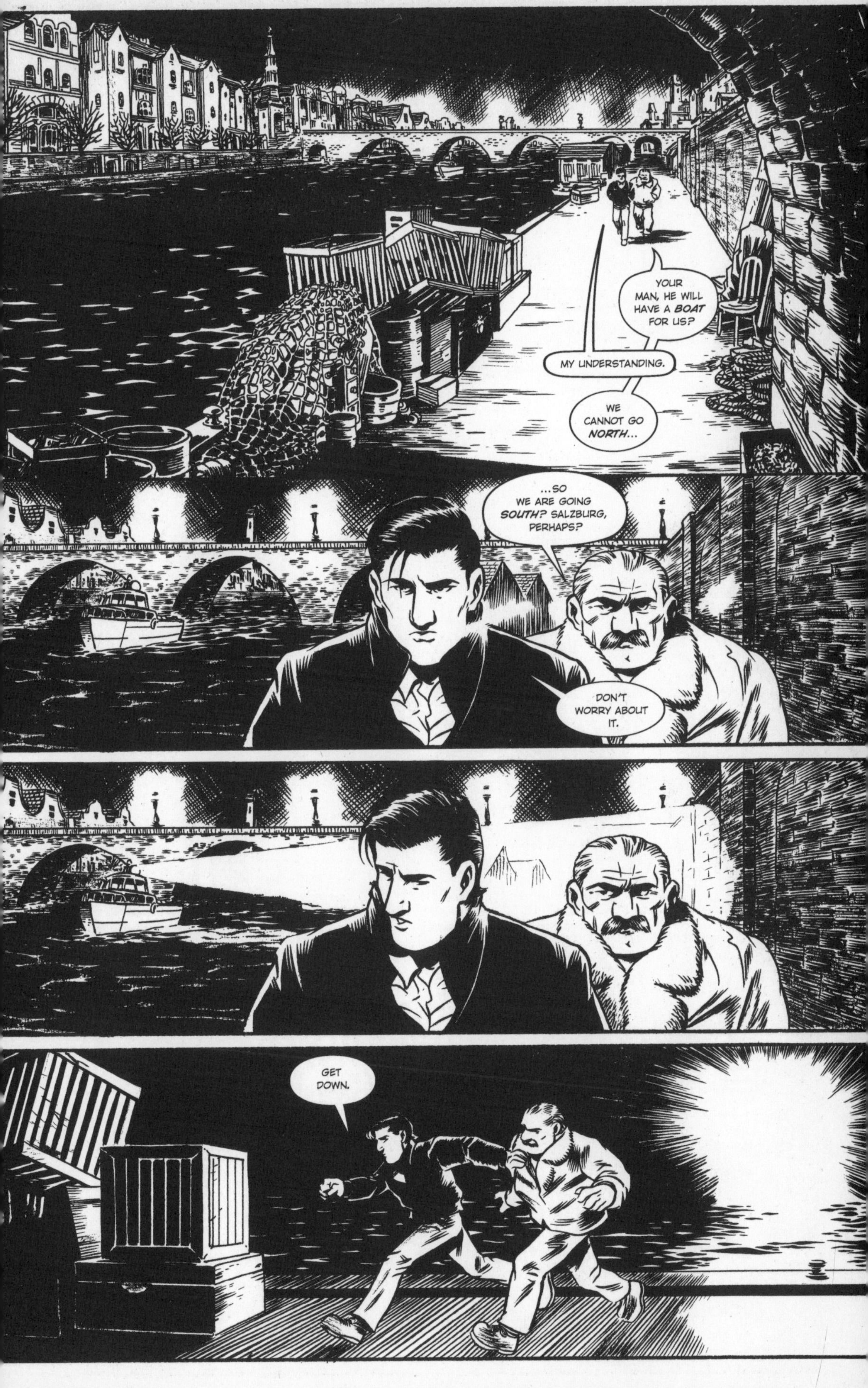
YOUR MAN, HE WILL HAVE A *BOAT* FOR US?
MY UNDERSTANDING.
WE CANNOT GO *NORTH*...
...SO WE ARE GOING *SOUTH?* SALZBURG, PERHAPS?
DON'T WORRY ABOUT IT.
GET DOWN.

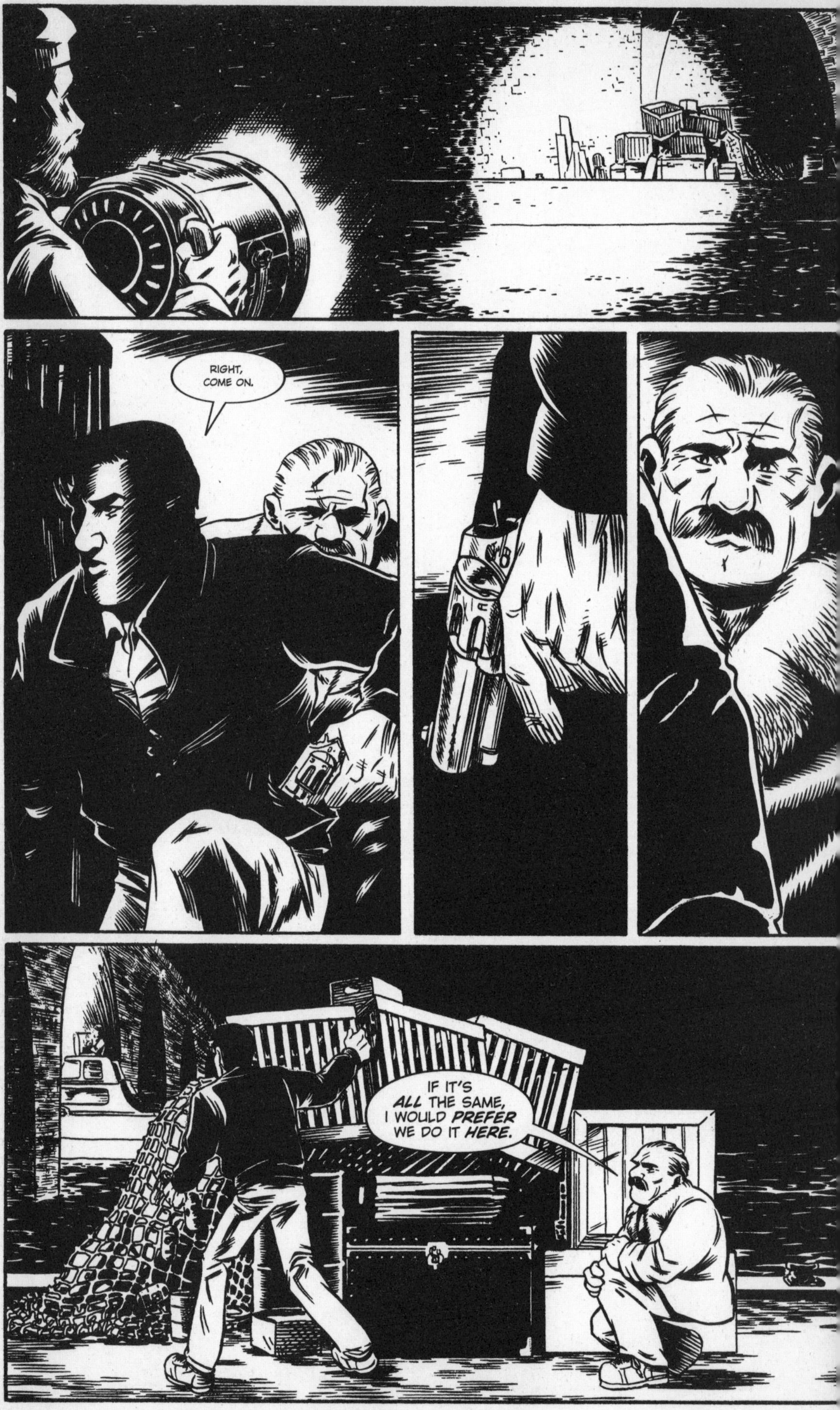
RIGHT, COME ON.
IF IT'S *ALL* THE SAME, I WOULD *PREFER* WE DO IT *HERE*.

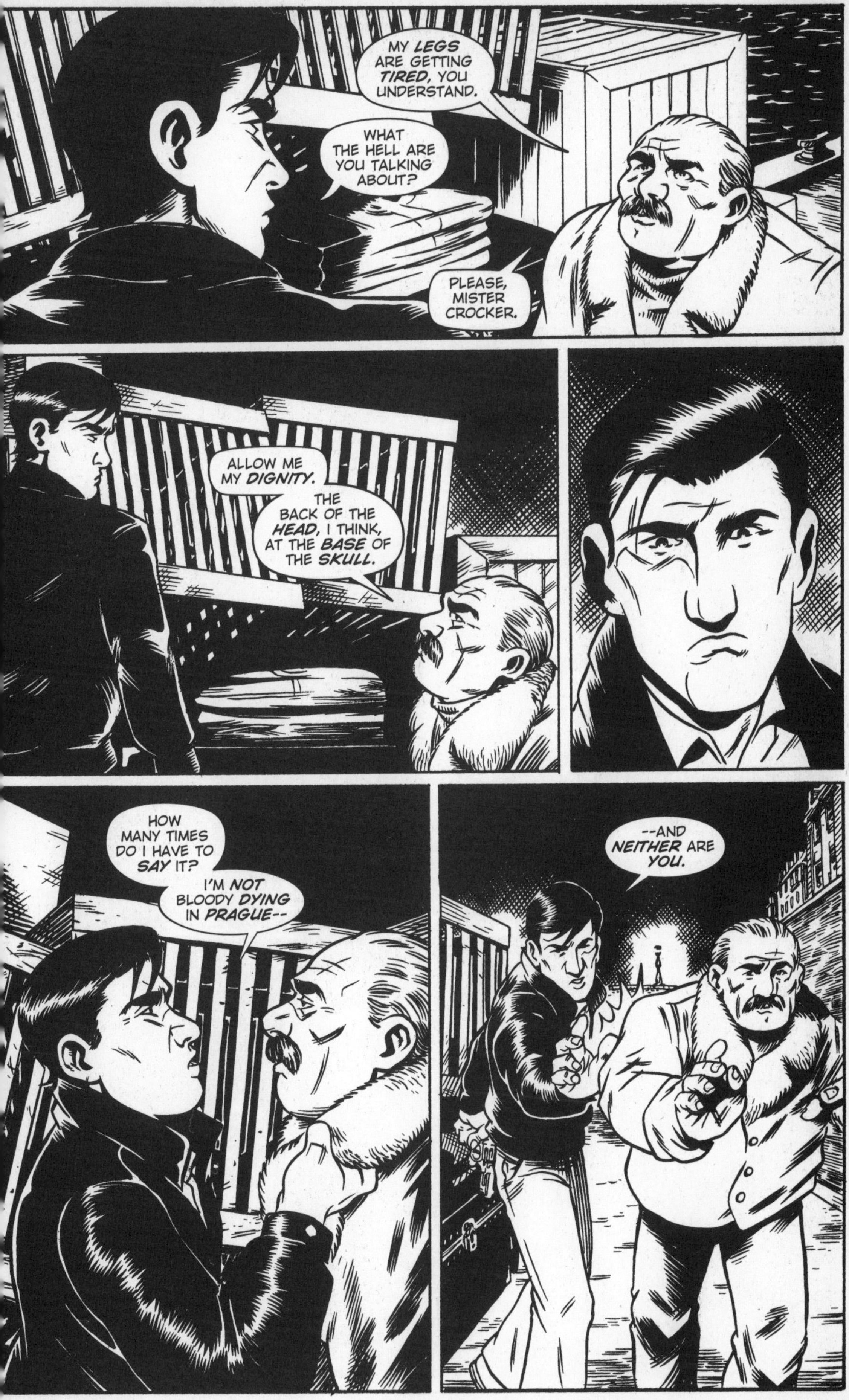

MY LEGS ARE GETTING TIRED, YOU UNDERSTAND.
WHAT THE HELL ARE YOU TALKING ABOUT?
PLEASE, MISTER CROCKER.
ALLOW ME MY DIGNITY.
THE BACK OF THE HEAD, I THINK, AT THE BASE OF THE SKULL.
HOW MANY TIMES DO I HAVE TO SAY IT?
I'M NOT BLOODY DYING IN PRAGUE--
--AND NEITHER ARE YOU.

WHERE'S THE CHARLES BRIDGE?

YOU'VE *PASSED* IT, IT'S NORTH OF HERE.

WE GOT *LOST*.

I'LL GIVE YOU A *LIFT*.

WE'D APPRECIATE IT.

HELP ME WITH THE *BOAT*.

YOU WERE SUPPOSED TO GET RID OF HIM.

CHANGE OF PLANS.

I WASN'T *PAID* FOR *THREE*.

THEN YOU CAN STAY *BEHIND*.

IT'S *MY* BOAT. IT'S *MY* RISK.

WE DON'T HAVE *TIME* FOR THIS.

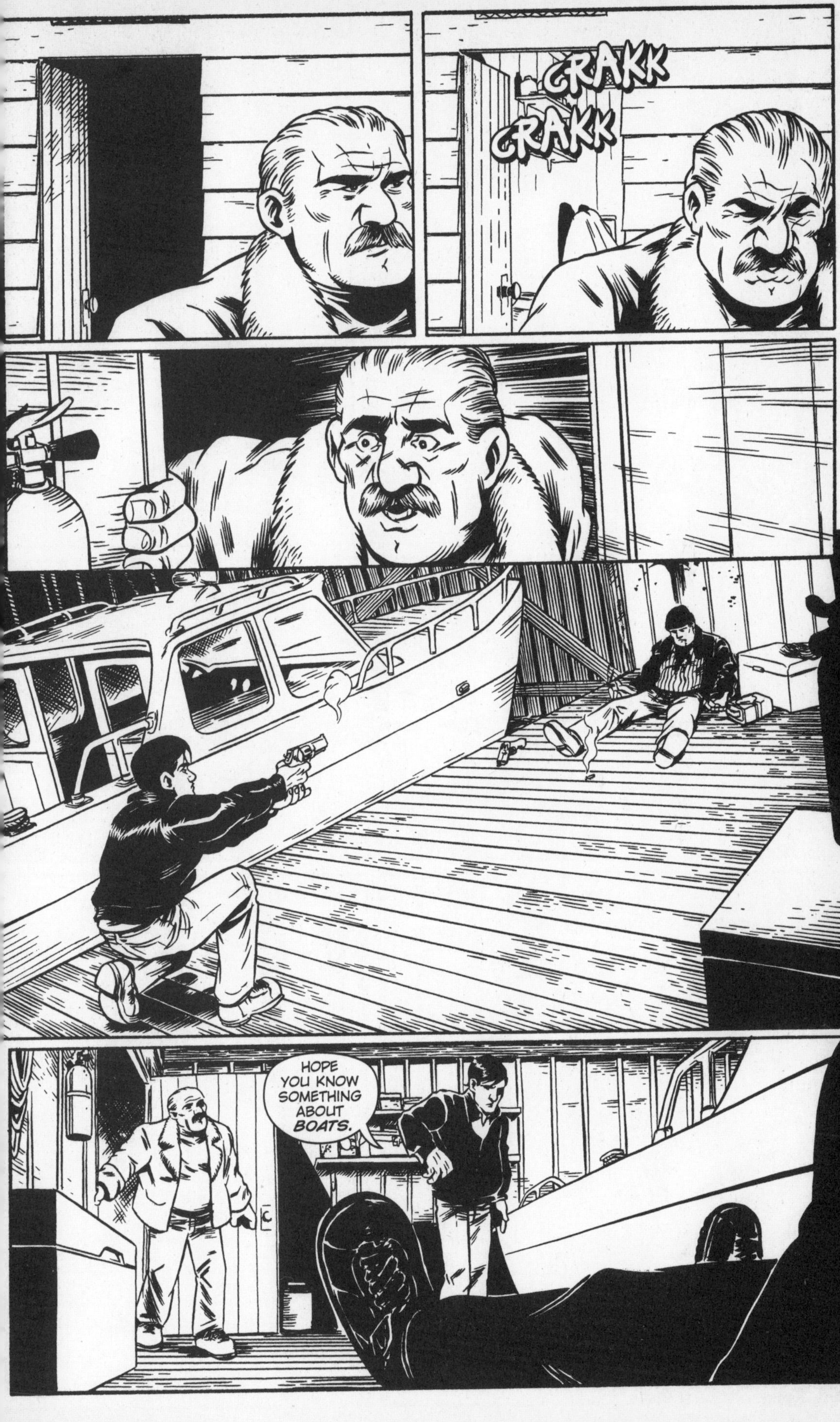
CRAKK
CRAKK
HOPE YOU KNOW SOMETHING ABOUT BOATS.

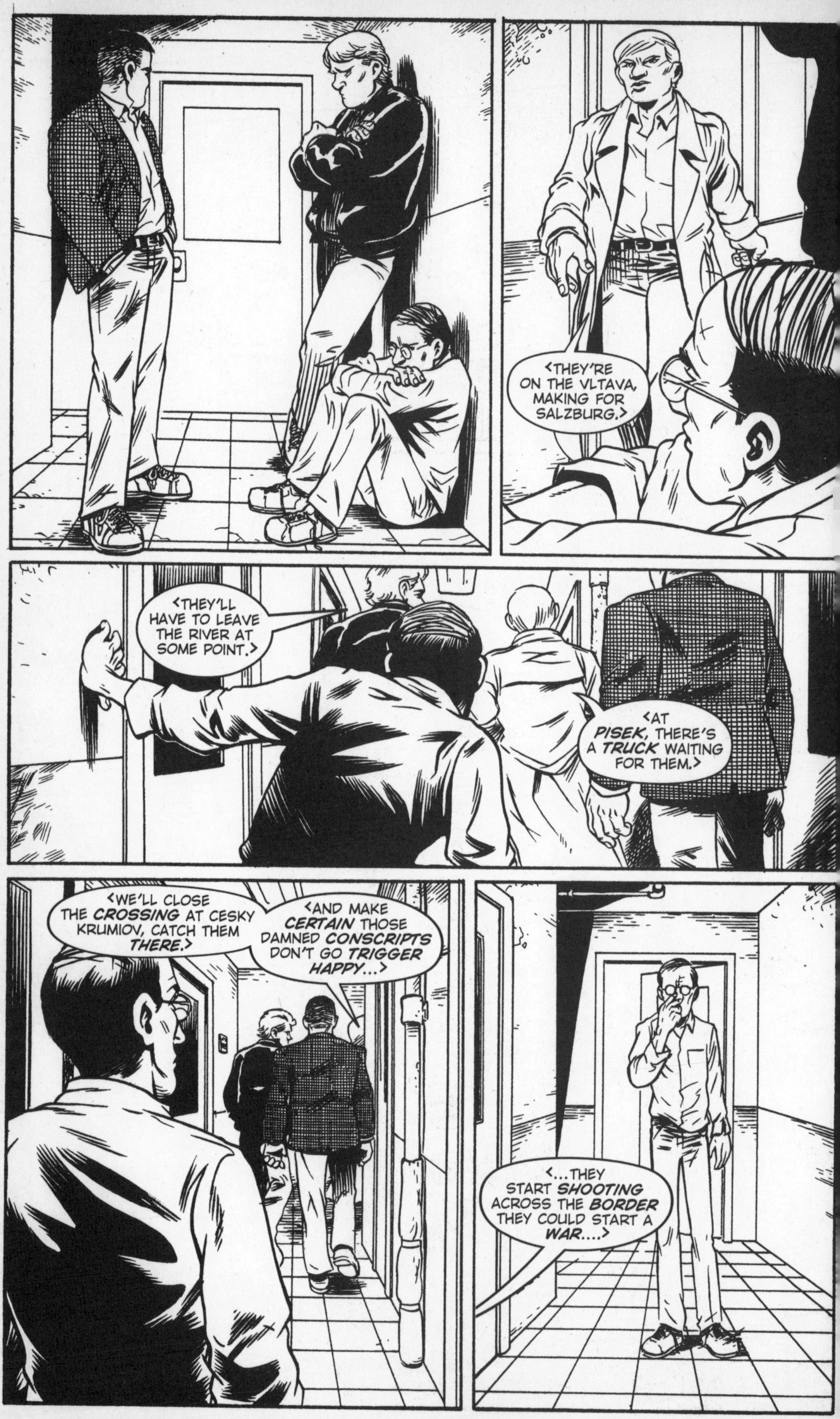

<THEY'RE ON THE VLTAVA, MAKING FOR SALZBURG.>
<THEY'LL HAVE TO LEAVE THE RIVER AT SOME POINT.>
<AT PISEK, THERE'S A TRUCK WAITING FOR THEM.>
<WE'LL CLOSE THE CROSSING AT CESKY KRUMIOV, CATCH THEM THERE.>
<AND MAKE CERTAIN THOSE DAMNED CONSCRIPTS DON'T GO TRIGGER HAPPY...>
<...THEY START SHOOTING ACROSS THE BORDER THEY COULD START A WAR....>

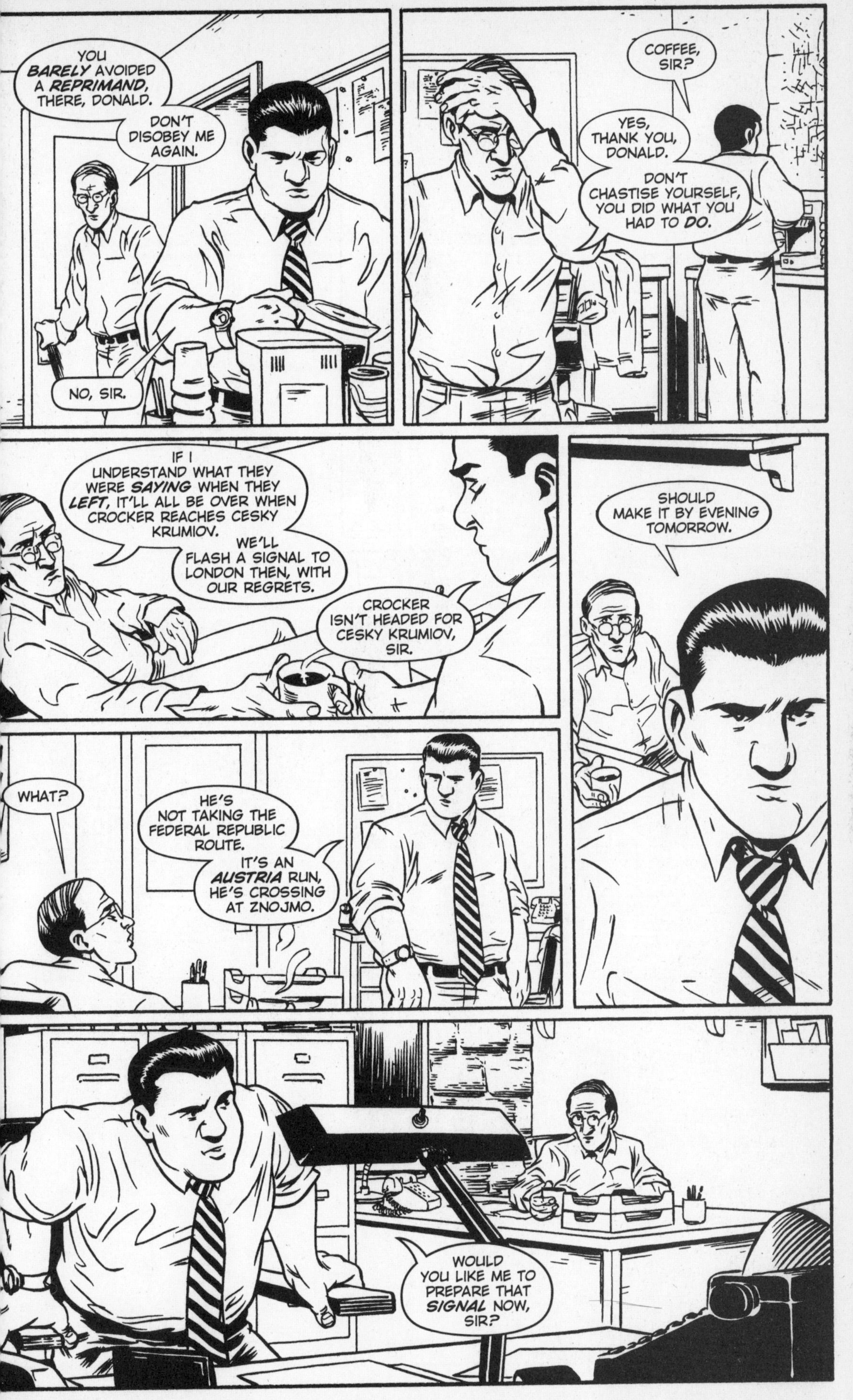
YOU *BARELY* AVOIDED A *REPRIMAND*, THERE, DONALD.
DON'T DISOBEY ME AGAIN.
NO, SIR.
COFFEE, SIR?
YES, THANK YOU, DONALD.
DON'T CHASTISE YOURSELF, YOU DID WHAT YOU HAD TO *DO*.
IF I UNDERSTAND WHAT THEY WERE *SAYING* WHEN THEY *LEFT*, IT'LL ALL BE OVER WHEN CROCKER REACHES CESKY KRUMIOV.
WE'LL FLASH A SIGNAL TO LONDON THEN, WITH OUR REGRETS.
CROCKER ISN'T HEADED FOR CESKY KRUMIOV, SIR.
SHOULD MAKE IT BY EVENING TOMORROW.
WHAT?
HE'S NOT TAKING THE FEDERAL REPUBLIC ROUTE.
IT'S AN *AUSTRIA* RUN, HE'S CROSSING AT ZNOJMO.
WOULD YOU LIKE ME TO PREPARE THAT *SIGNAL* NOW, SIR?

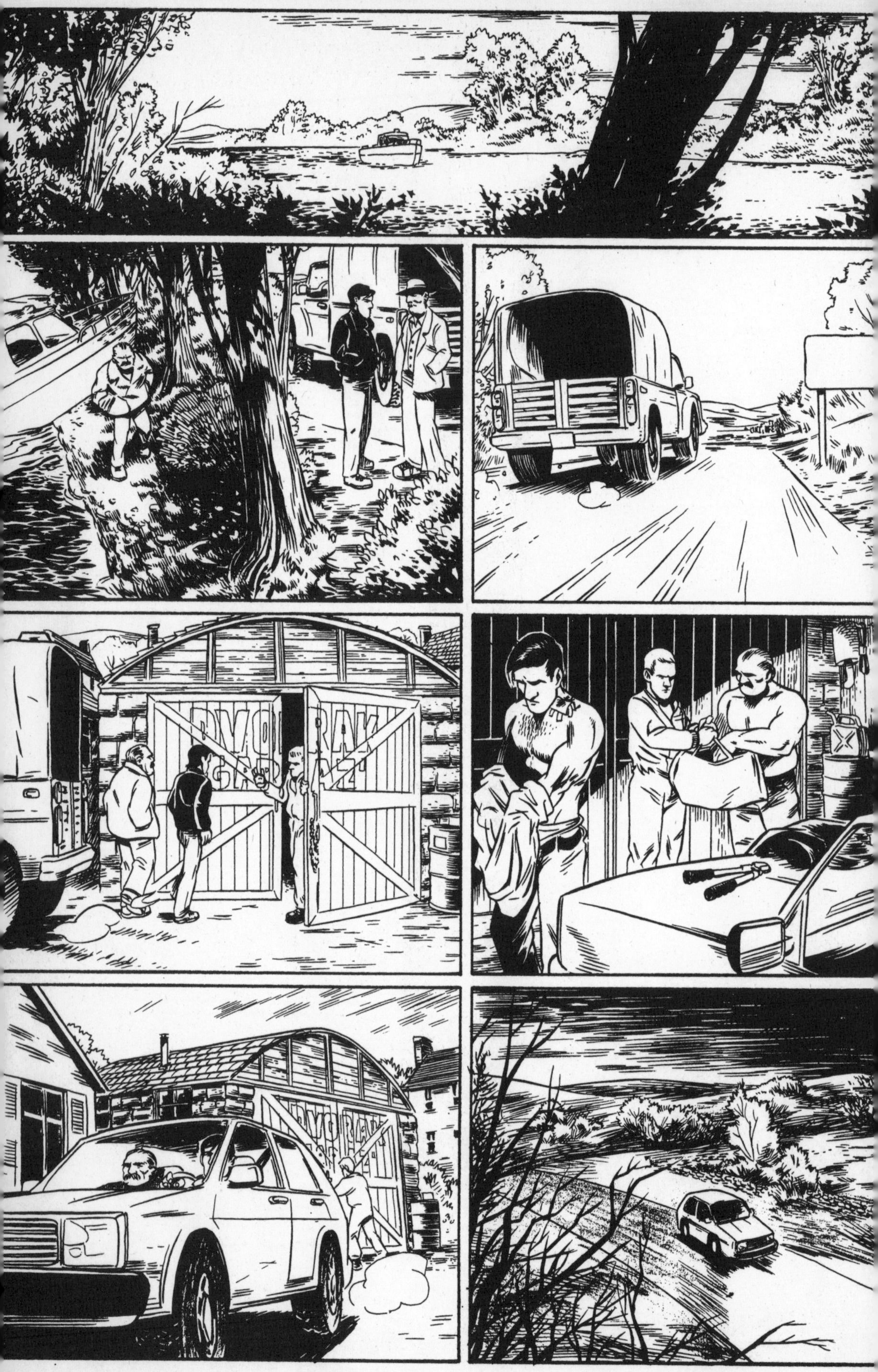
DVORAK

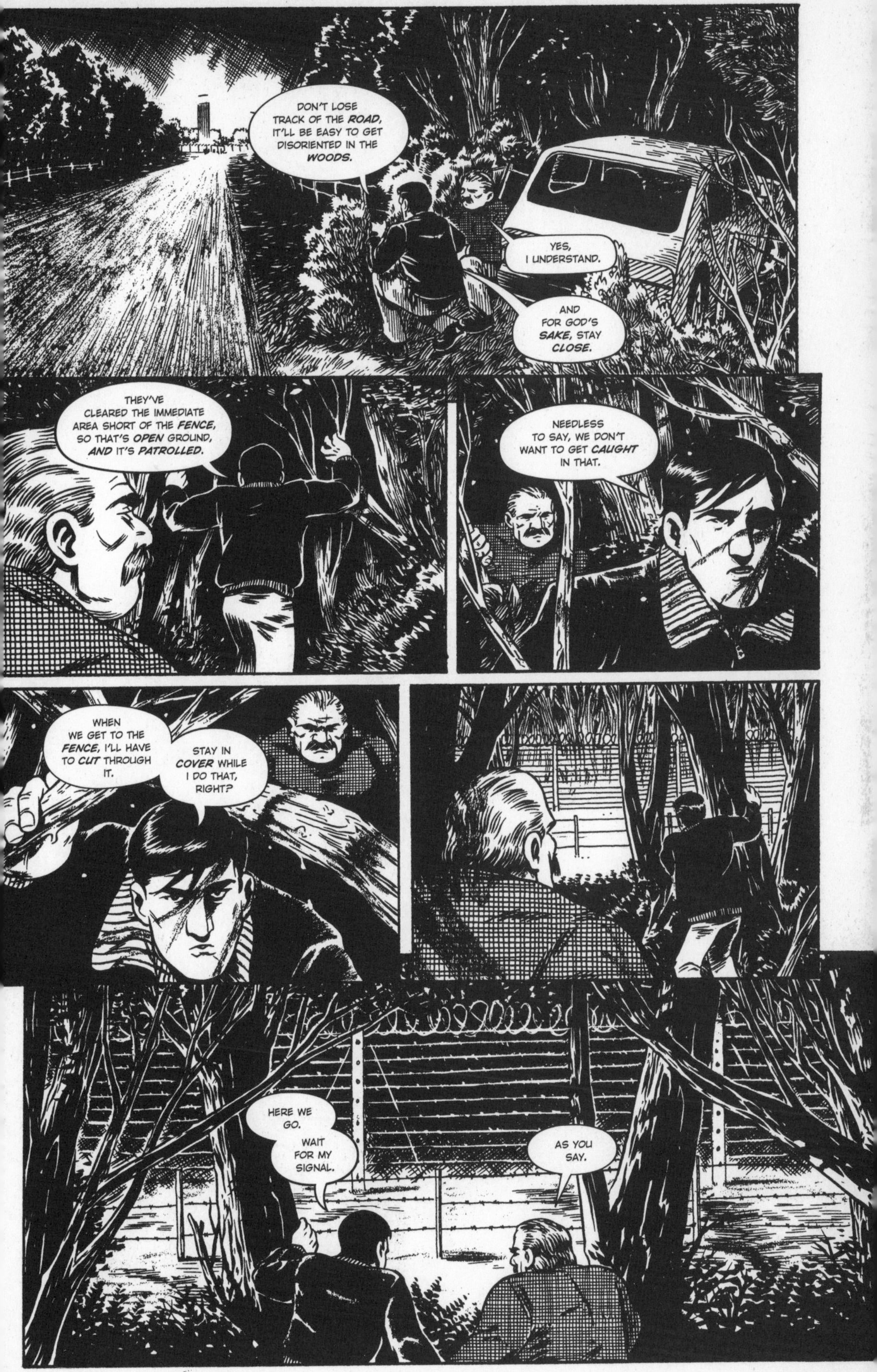
DON'T LOSE TRACK OF THE ROAD, IT'LL BE EASY TO GET DISORIENTED IN THE WOODS.
YES, I UNDERSTAND.
AND FOR GOD'S SAKE, STAY CLOSE.
THEY'VE CLEARED THE IMMEDIATE AREA SHORT OF THE FENCE, SO THAT'S OPEN GROUND, AND IT'S PATROLLED.
NEEDLESS TO SAY, WE DON'T WANT TO GET CAUGHT IN THAT.
WHEN WE GET TO THE FENCE, I'LL HAVE TO CUT THROUGH IT.
STAY IN COVER WHILE I DO THAT, RIGHT?
HERE WE GO.
WAIT FOR MY SIGNAL.
AS YOU SAY.

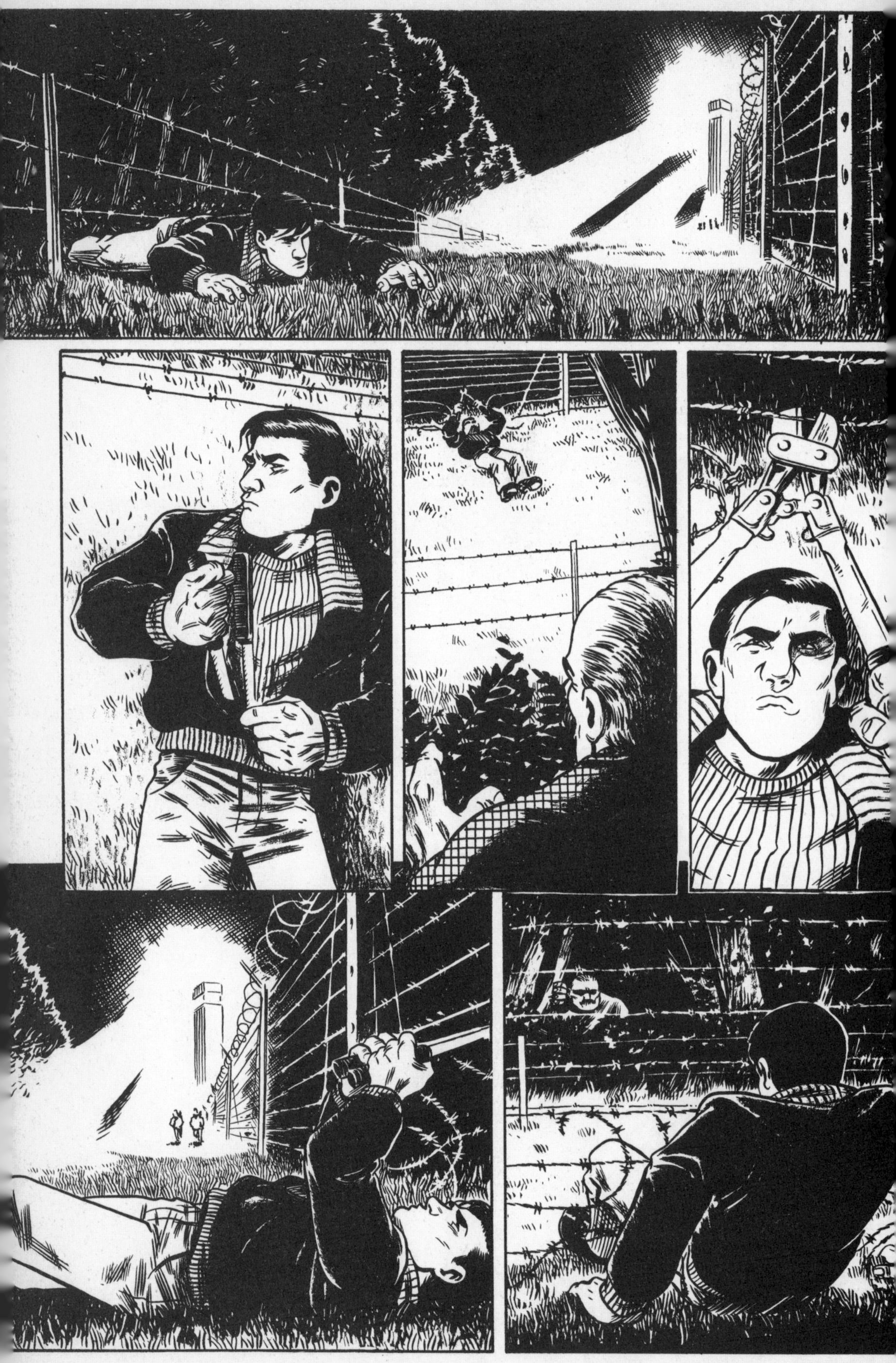

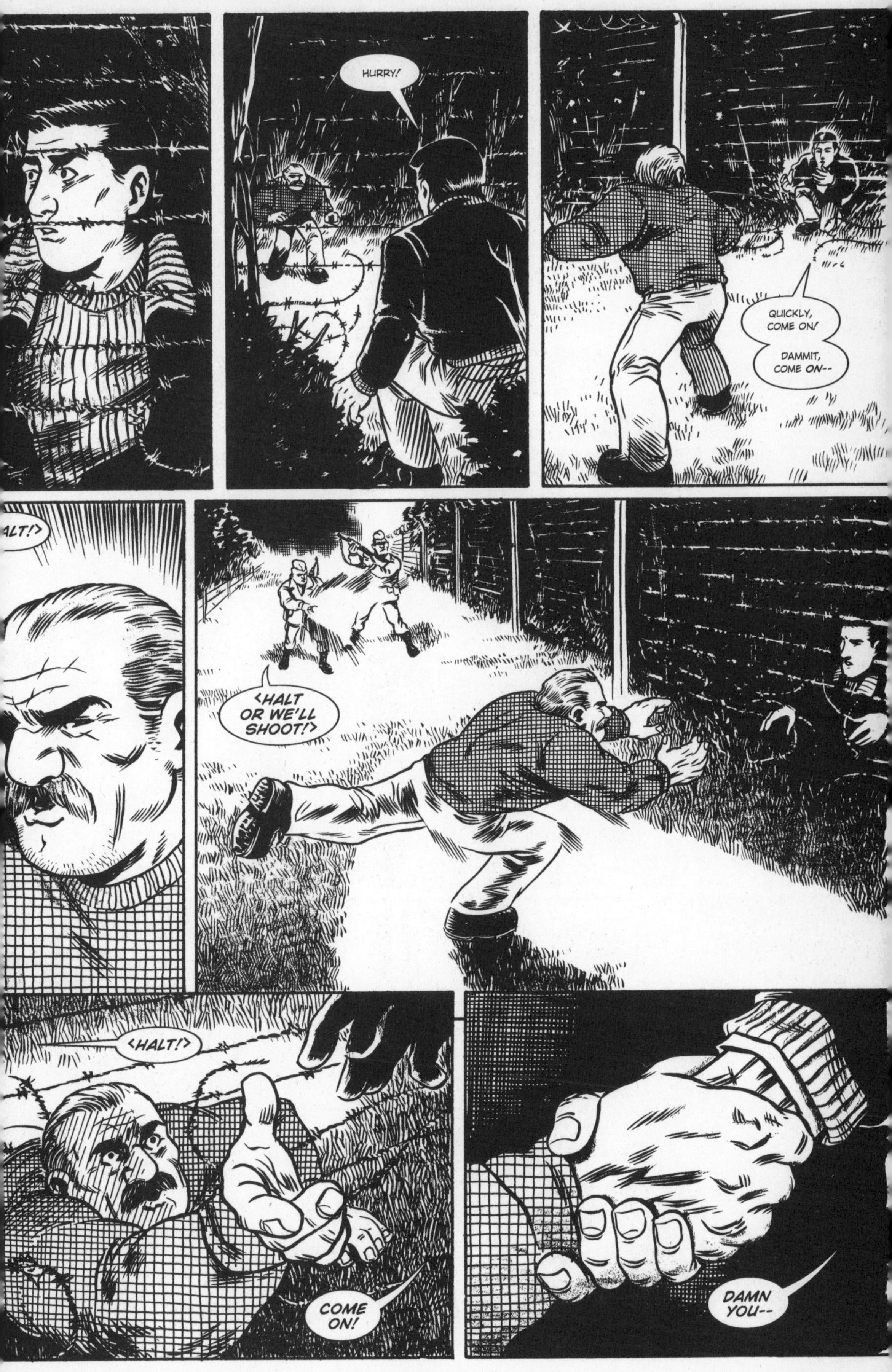
HURRY!
QUICKLY, COME ON!
DAMMIT, COME ON--
<HALT!>
<HALT OR WE'LL SHOOT!>
<HALT!>
COME ON!
DAMN YOU--

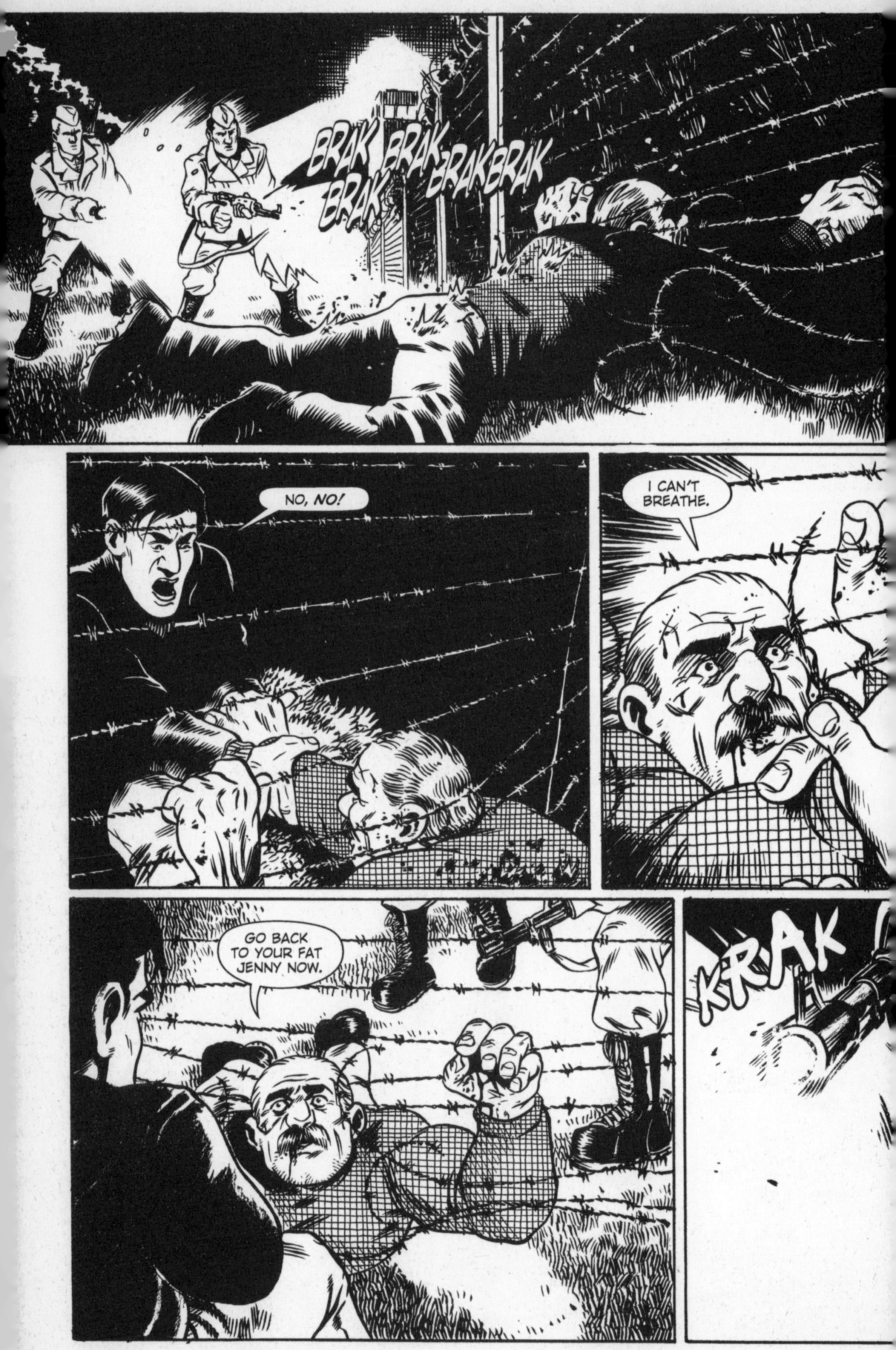
BRAK BRAK BRAK BRAKBRAK BRAK
NO, NO!
I CAN'T BREATHE.
GO BACK TO YOUR FAT JENNY NOW.
KRAK

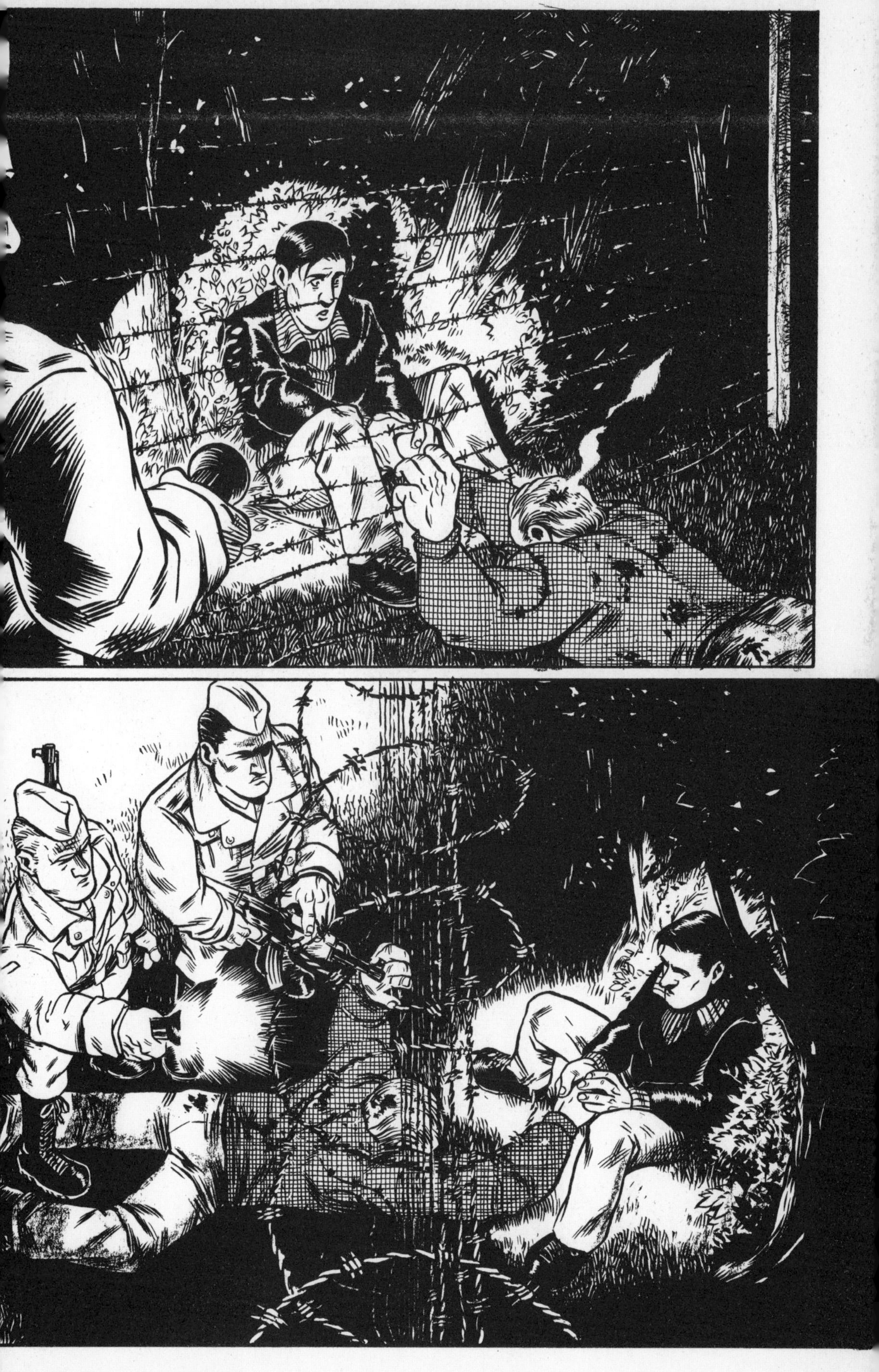

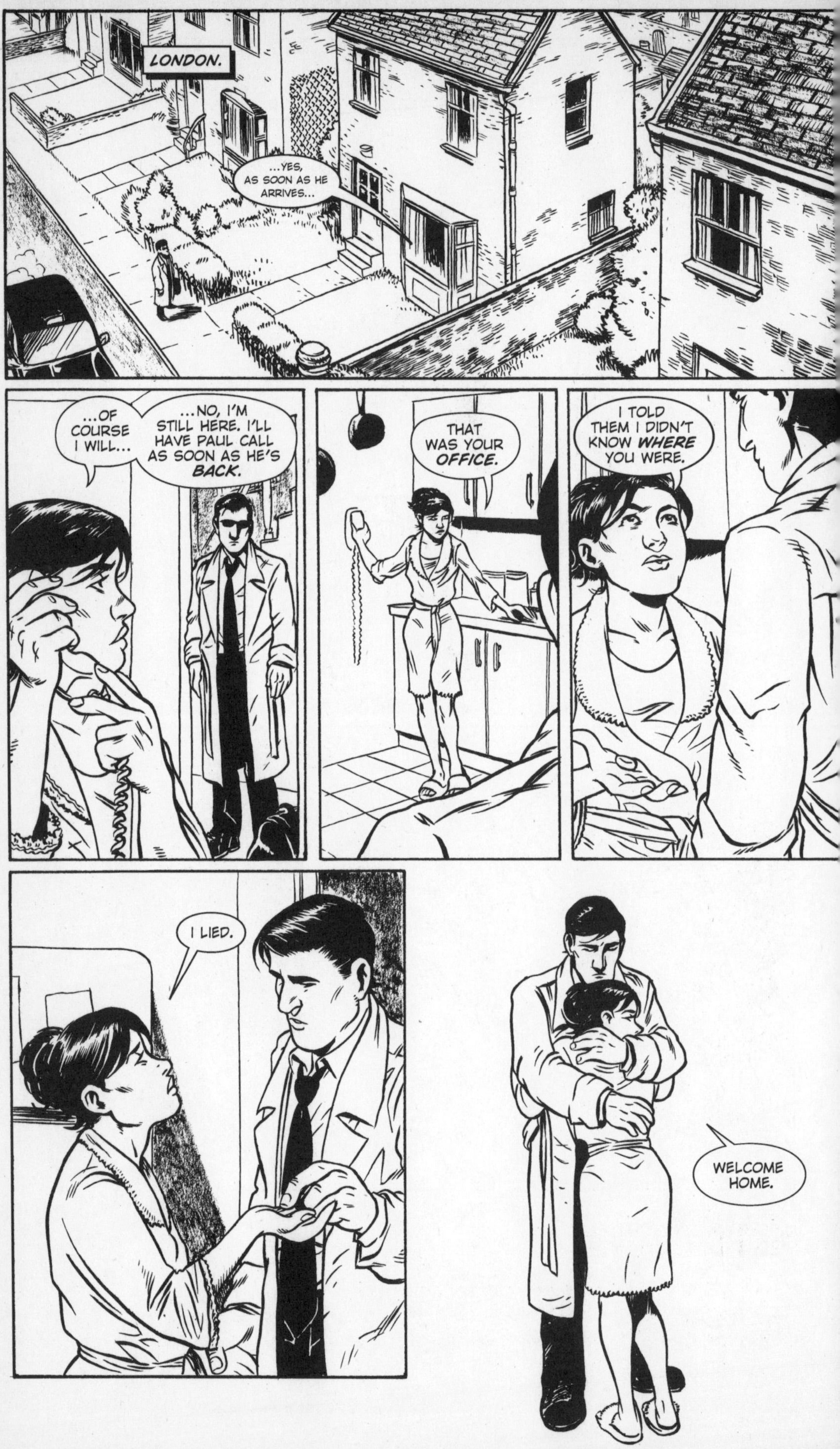
LONDON.
...YES, AS SOON AS HE ARRIVES...
...OF COURSE I WILL...
...NO, I'M STILL HERE. I'LL HAVE PAUL CALL AS SOON AS HE'S BACK.
THAT WAS YOUR OFFICE.
I TOLD THEM I DIDN'T KNOW WHERE YOU WERE.
I LIED.
WELCOME HOME.

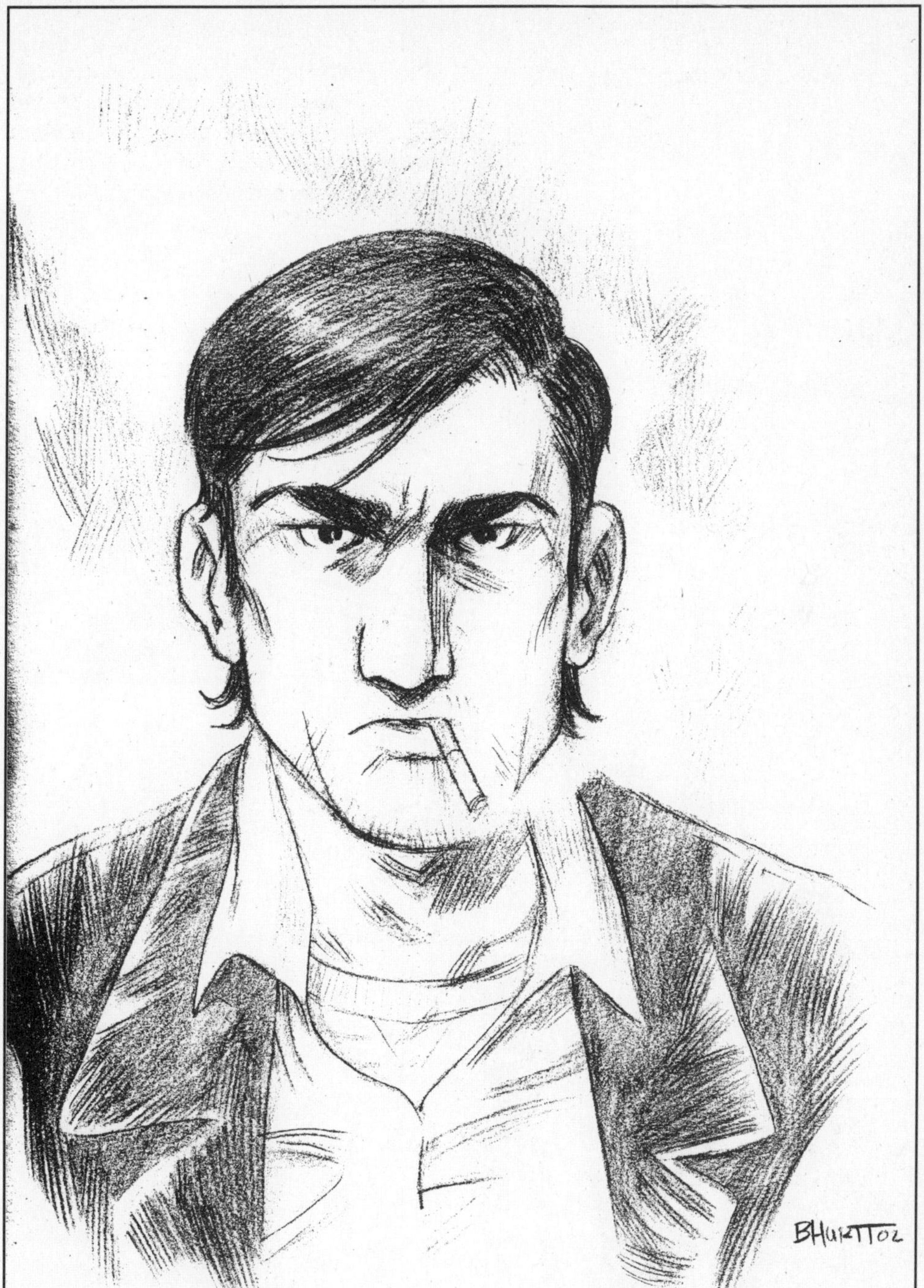
BHURTT02

BASIC TRAINING

Queen & Country – Operation: Morningstar *artist Brian Hurtt was the one who initially urged Greg to take this look at Crocker's past. The material on the following pages includes his initial designs for Paul, as well as a look at his approach to individual story pages.*

CAFE OHEN

Brian Hurtt's pencils for a page of chapter two, followed by a rough panel layout. Notice how Brian plans his panels for camera placement and shadow before he ever starts drawing on the actual boards.

ALL BLEED ART MUST EXTEND TO SOLID LINE

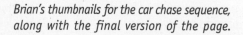

Brian's thumbnails for the car chase sequence, along with the final version of the page.

Brian's early sketches for three different versions of Crocker: showing the stress of the job, cartoon Crocker from the wild imagination of Mr. Hurtt, and the eager Crocker from the early pages of this book.

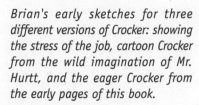

From these panels, you can see the attention to detail Brian pays to his action sequences even in the earliest stages.

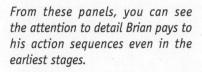

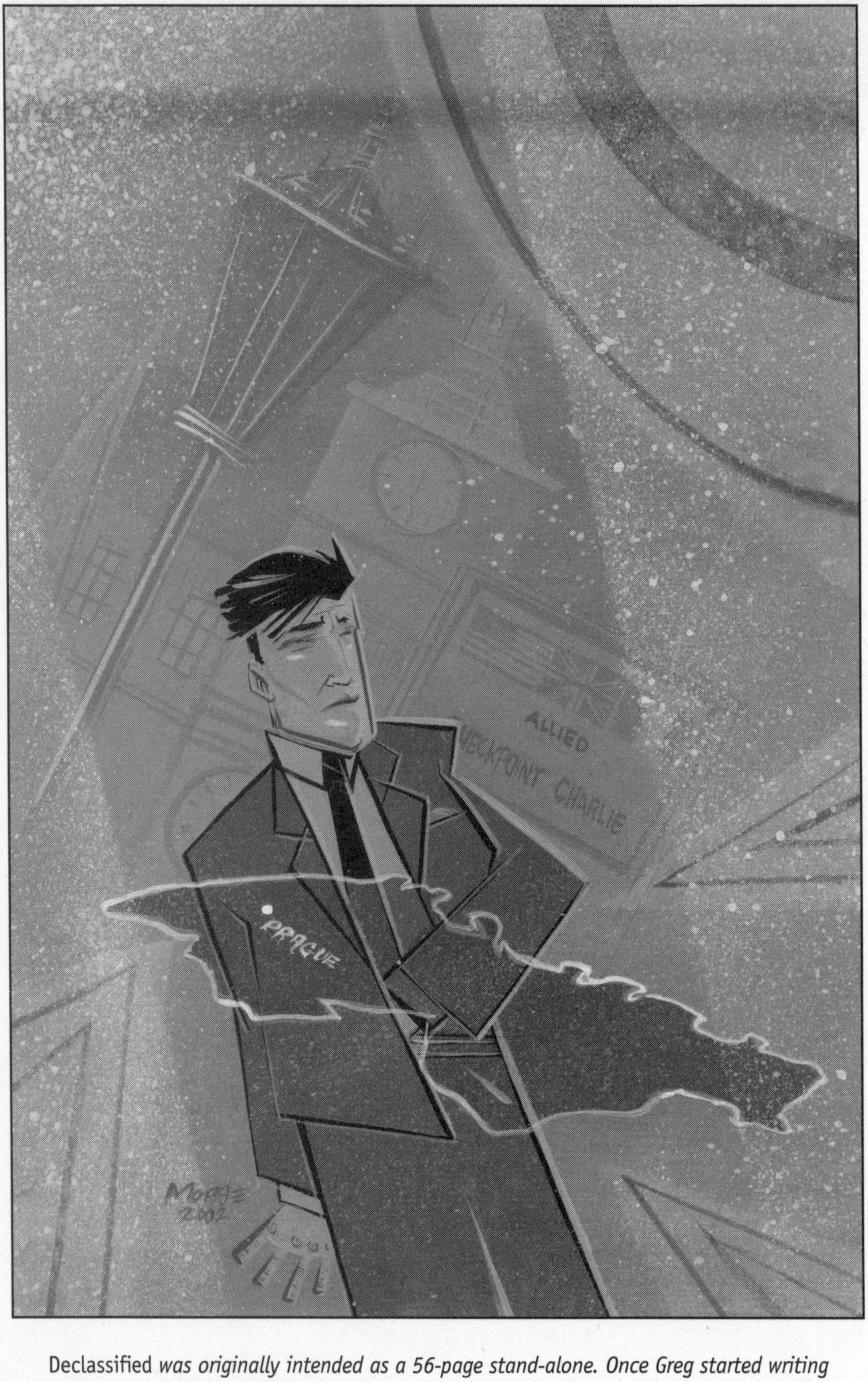
ALLIED
CHECKPOINT CHARLIE
PRAGUE
MORSE
2002

Declassified *was originally intended as a 56-page stand-alone. Once Greg started writing though, the script took on a life of its own and became this weightier volume. Above is cover artist Scott Morse's original cover for the story which was discarded when Scott decided to use specific design elements on all three covers.*

GREG RUCKA

Born in San Francisco, Greg Rucka was raised on the Monterey Peninsula. He is the author of several novels, including four about bodyguard Atticus Kodiak, and of numerous comic books. He has won two Eisner Awards for his work in the field, including one for *Whiteout: Melt* (Best Limited Series, 2000) and one for *Queen & Country* (Best New Series, 2002). His most recent writing credits for comics include *Gotham Central*, the newly relaunched *Wolverine*, and a much-anticipated tenure on the monthly *Wonder Woman* title. Greg resides in Portland, Oregon, with his wife, Jennifer; their son, Elliot; and their daughter, Dashiell. His next novel, *A Fistful of Rain*, is due in July 2003, and he is planning a miniseries about an expedition to climb Mt. Everest to be drawn by Scott Morse.

BRIAN HURTT

Brian Hurtt was born in Wichita, KS, and since then has traveled the world, only recently settling down in St. Louis, MO. He began his career in comics in 2001, debuting as the second penciller of *Queen & Country*. He has since collaborated with the writing team of Nunzio DeFilippis and Christina Weir, first on the critically acclaimed thriller *Skinwalker*, then on the socially conscious *Three Strikes*. He recently completed drawing a special stand-alone issue of DC's *Gotham Central* series and is now preparing for a new ongoing assignment in mainstream comics.

Other books by GREG RUCKA...

GREG RUCKA
STEVE LIEBER

Whiteout™
by Greg Rucka &
Steve Lieber
128 pages, b&w interiors
$11.95 US
ISBN 0-9667127-1-4

WHITEOUT
MELT

Whiteout: Melt™
by Greg Rucka &
Steve Lieber
128 pages, b&w interiors
$11.95 US
ISBN 1-929998-03-1

QUEEN & COUNTRY
GREG RUCKA · STEVE ROLSTON

***Queen & Counry*™ Vol. 1 Operation: Broken Ground**
by Greg Rucka, Steve
Rolston & Stan Sakai
128 pages, b&w interiors
$11.95 US
ISBN 1-929998-21-X

QUEEN & COUNTRY

***Queen & Counry*™ Vol. 2 Operation: Morningstar**
by Rucka, Hurtt,
O'Malley & Norrie
88 pages, b&w interiors
$8.95 US
ISBN 1-929998-35-X

QUEEN & COUNTRY

***Queen & Counry*™ Vol. 3 Operation: Crystal Ball**
by Greg Rucka, &
Leandro Fernandez
88 pages, b&w interiors
$14.95 US
ISBN 1-929998-49-X

***"Whiteout's** well researched, well written and expertly rendered. Don't buy it for those reasons, though. Buy it because Carrie Stetko's mouthy, freckled and cool..."*
– Kelly Sue DeConnick, artbomb.net

"Greg Rucka is not a lesser writer. As an author, he thrives in political, moral and emotional complexity."
– Warren Ellis, creator of **Transmetropolitan** *and* **Global Frequency**

THE ATTICUS KODIAK
Novels from Bantam Books...

CRITICAL
SPACE
GREG RUCKA

Critical Space
hardcover edition
$23.95 US
ISBN 0-553-80132-5

KEEPER
GREG RUCKA

Keeper
$5.99 US
ISBN 0-553-57428-0

FINDER
"A top-notch thriller... a powerhouse of a story that will leave readers gasping."
GREG RUCKA

Finder
$5.99 US
ISBN 0-553-57429-9

"A MEGATHRILLER
smoker
THERE IS ONLY ONE WAY
TO KEEP A WITNESS FROM TESTIFYING
GREG RUCKA

Smoker
$5.99 US
ISBN 0-553-57829-4

shooting
at
midnight
GREG RUCKA

Shooting At Midnight
$5.99 US
ISBN 0-553-57827-8

"Rucka blends Spillaine's 'tough-guy' private eye with Chandler's noir insights and Hemingway's Spartan expression..."
– Statesman Journal, Salem, Oregon

AVAILABLE AT FINER BOOKSTORES EVERYWHERE

For a comics store near you,
call **1-888-COMIC-BOOK**
or visit **www.the-master-list.com**.

For more information on more
Oni Press books go to:
www.onipress.com

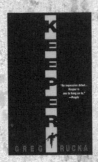